2.96

DATE DUE

MR 11'98			
AP 30'98			

712-347-5492

MATT CHRISTOPHER

On the Court with...
Andre Agassi

Little, Brown and Company
Boston   New York   Toronto   London

To Chuck Howell

Copyright ©1997 by Matthew F. Christopher

First Edition

Cover photograph by Ron Angle, Sports Illustrated/© Time Inc.

Library of Congress Cataloging-in-Publication Data

Christopher, Matt.
    Andre Agassi: on the court with / Matt Christopher. — 1st. ed.
      p.   cm.
    Summary: A biography of the talented and colorful tennis player who earned the number one ranking in 1995.
    ISBN 0-316-14202-6 (pbk.)
    1. Agassi, Andre, 1970–   — Juvenile literature.   Tennis players—United States — Biography — Juvenile literature.
    [1. Agassi, Andre, 1970– . 2. Tennis players.]   I. Title.
GV994.A43C57   1997
796.342′092 — dc21
 [B]   96-46618

10 9 8 7 6 5 4 3 2 1

COM-MO

Published simultaneously in Canada by Little, Brown & Company (Canada) Limited

Printed in the United States of America

Contents

Prologue

The serve is a blazing blur, flying across the net at 130 miles per hour. To the crowd in the stands, it looks like an ace, or at least a sure winner.

But no — with lightning-quick reflexes, the player on the other side of the net pivots, hits a two-fisted backhand, and sends a sizzling return across the net! The ball hits the line, sending up a cloud of chalk powder. The server can only stare at the spot in disbelief, as the crowd erupts in a tremendous roar. Their hero has done it again!

Game . . . set . . . match . . . Andre Agassi.

Chapter One

A Passion for the Game

Andre Agassi's rise to the top of the men's tennis world began before he was even born. In fact, his father, Emmanuel "Mike" Agassi, was just a boy himself when the tennis bug first bit the Agassi family.

Emmanuel was born in 1932 in Teheran, the capital of Iran, to a poor Armenian merchant family. He lived in a dangerous neighborhood, and at a very early age he had to use his fists to protect himself from older, bigger boys. He learned quickly that life was harsh and that you had to be a fighter to survive. It was a lesson that shaped his whole life — and the lives of his children, too.

In 1941 the United States sent troops into Iran to support the shah, or king, when his power was threatened by rebels. Young Emmanuel climbed the wall of the American Mission church one day to escape from the fights and the heat to the cool, peaceful shade of the courtyard. There he saw a strange sight that fascinated him — two American soldiers hitting a ball back and forth to each other over a net with rackets. The rackets were old, and the soldiers weren't very good players, but they seemed to be having a good time.

Seeing the ragged little boy, the soldiers beckoned him over. They made friends with Emmanuel, with gifts of chocolate and gum. Emmanuel began to hang around the homemade tennis court regularly, watching the game with rapt attention. One day, the soldiers gave him a present — an old wooden racket they'd restrung with fuse wire. They taught him how to use it and would hit the ball back and forth with him once in a while. In return, Emmanuel became their ball-boy — retrieving tennis balls and pushing the hand-roller over the court to flatten the dirt surface.

That was the beginning of Emmanuel Agassi's lifelong love affair with tennis. He was good at the game right away, and quickly became better. Yet Emmanuel was to rise to national fame not with a tennis

4

racket but with his fists. In 1948 he went to London to represent Iran in the Summer Olympics as a middleweight boxer.

Emmanuel Agassi did not like boxing particularly. Tennis was his passion. But there weren't very many sports heroes in Iran in those days, and suddenly, the whole nation was talking about the possibility of Emmanuel Agassi's winning a gold medal. Boxing, it seemed, might provide him with a way out of poverty.

Unfortunately, Agassi stepped into the ring in London against Lazslo Papp of Hungary, the man who would go on to become champion of Europe. Emmanuel Agassi, and Iran's hopes for Olympic gold, were quickly dashed.

The seventeen-year-old had nothing to do until the closing ceremonies. So one day, Emmanuel took a train out to Wimbledon, in South London. Wimbledon is the home of the famous All England Tennis Club, the most hallowed place in the entire tennis world. There, every year, the oldest, greatest tennis tournament of them all takes place — the Championship of All England, better known simply as "Wimbledon."

Young Emmanuel stared from outside the gates at

the limousines and fancy cars that rode on through. He daydreamed that one day they would be coming to see him play. Of course, it was only a dream. The next week he was back in Iran, and Wimbledon seemed a million miles away.

In 1952 he again represented his country in the Olympics, this time in Helsinki, Finland, as a heavyweight. He lost to America's Floyd Patterson, who went on to become World Champion.

By this time, Emmanuel Agassi had made a fateful decision — he would leave Iran for America, for the great city of Chicago, where many Armenians had already settled. There, he would try to make his name as a professional boxer.

In his first three years in Chicago, Emmanuel became a Golden Gloves amateur champion. But his goal was to make money from his fights, and he could not do that as an amateur. Then, one day, a promoter from New York called. He thought he could sell Emmanuel as "The Fighting Armenian." Emmanuel agreed, so the promoter booked him into Madison Square Garden to fight an easy opponent.

Emmanuel, who had by now changed his name to "Mike," was excited. It was his first professional fight! True, he wasn't crazy about boxing. But this fight, an easy one, would be good money. Soon, he fantasized, he would become famous.

Unfortunately — or maybe fortunately — the "easy" opponent got sick with a high fever on the night of the fight. He was replaced at the last minute by a fighter who had fifty bouts under his belt and was feared for his murderous right hand.

Mike Agassi had not bargained for this, and he was terrified. Saying he had to go to the locker room, he proceeded to squeeze through the window and escape. Soon he was on a train back to Chicago. Along the way, he threw his boxing gloves out the window, promising himself he would never get into the ring again.

Since he wasn't going to be a boxer anymore, twenty-three-year-old Mike Agassi had to find a new line of work. He went through several jobs, looking for the right one for him. In the meantime, he picked up tennis again, playing on his neighborhood asphalt courts.

Whenever Mike would play, crowds would gather to cheer and applaud. Not only was he good, but he played the game differently from everyone else.

Tennis in the 1950s was a genteel, polite game. But when Mike Agassi played, he approached tennis the way he approached boxing — get in there and hit as ferociously as you can.

Mike was a true tennis fanatic. He would play in pouring rain. When it snowed, he would get out the shovel, clear the court, and drag some poor soul out to play a set with him.

Eventually, he found a job with a local construction company that built houses for rich people, complete with swimming pools and tennis courts. Mike Agassi's only interest, of course, was the last part. He made it his business to learn everything he could about how tennis courts were built and maintained. He learned so much that he soon knew more than his boss.

Always ready for a fight, Mike began arguing whenever he felt his boss was doing something wrong. The boss didn't like being argued with, and Mike was soon unemployed again. But at least he'd learned something of lasting value. He now knew that tennis was the true love of his life.

Mike's next job was as a trainee waiter at the posh Ambassador Hotel. There, one night, he helped serve at a special dinner for the finalist Davis Cup teams of the United States and Australia. The Davis Cup is the world championship of team tennis, and the best players of many nations compete for their countries.

Mike Agassi watched the two coaches toast each other's players. He heard the Australian coach say that tennis talent had to be nurtured and coached from as young an age as possible. Agassi promised himself that someday a son of his would be sitting at just such a table, before his own Davis Cup final match.

By this time Mike had gotten married, and he and his wife, Betty, had three small children: Rita, Phillip, and Tamra. And despite the fact that he had a job waiting tables now at a good hotel, Mike was unhappy with life in Chicago. It was too cold there, and it was impossible to play tennis year-round. He decided to pack his family up and take off for the West Coast, where the weather was warm, the sun always shone, and tennis players grew in bunches.

But there was no work in Los Angeles, Mike soon discovered. On the way out to Los Angeles, he had seen all the big hotels in Las Vegas, with their fine tennis courts and highly paid tennis instructors. Mike's experience as a waiter would surely land him a job. So he packed the family into the station wagon and headed east again.

Soon the Agassi family was settled in Las Vegas. Betty got a job with the Nevada State Employment Agency, and Mike found work as a waiter in the casinos.

Mike gradually worked his way up to the position of showroom captain at Caesar's Palace, one of the grandest casino-hotels on the Las Vegas strip. It is the job of the showroom captain to escort ticket-holders to their seats. It's up to him where he seats people, and the bigger the tip, the better the seat.

Some of the greatest names in the entertainment world come to perform in Las Vegas. Championship boxing matches take place there, too. Mike met and became friendly with many of the stars and boxing champions. He also got to meet the world-class tennis players who came to play exhibition matches in the fourteen-thousand-seat tennis stadium at Caesar's Palace.

Mike had also begun teaching tennis, and soon he opened his own racket-restringing business. It was very successful, thanks to Mike's tennis know-how and his big-name contacts. The Agassis were doing very well indeed. And their family was still growing. On April 29, 1970, their fourth child, Andre, was born.

Chapter Two
1970-1972

Born with a Racket in His Hand

Unlike baseball, basketball, football, or hockey, tennis is an individual sport. You don't have your whole team to back you up if you make a mistake or are having a bad day. In baseball, if you're not hitting, your pitcher can still throw a shutout and your team can win. In tennis, if your serve has taken the day off, you're through. And when the press writes about what happened, there's no one else to share the burden of losing or the pressure of winning next time.

Mike Agassi's dreams for his children meant that from the very first, they were surrounded by tennis. Mike had rigged several ball machines on the hotel courts so that his children could practice every day. Other machines pushed the balls to the side of the court, collected them, and reloaded them into the ball machines.

Mike hadn't forgotten what he'd overheard at the Ambassador Hotel in Chicago about starting future tennis stars young. From the time Rita, Phillip, and Tami were three years old, they were hitting a thousand balls a day. Mike would work at the casino till three A.M., then rise at seven to wake the kids and shepherd them onto the tennis court for an hour of practice before school.

For Mike, tennis was the ticket to a better life for his children. So he insisted on their practicing every day for hours. Only on the rare rainy day in Las Vegas would the children get a break. "We used to pray for rain," one of them remembered later.

The two oldest children were the "guinea pigs" for Mike's champion-molding teaching method. He would often yell at them, trying to get them to improve their game. If the kids didn't make it to the finals of their tournaments, he would humiliate them. He thought that if they hated losing enough, it would help them win.

Rita was the oldest, and a talented player. But she couldn't take the relentless approach her father used. She developed a fearsome two-handed backhand stroke, like the one later made famous by Monica

Seles. But she also developed health problems from all the stress. One day, after losing a match in a national tournament, she left the court vomiting blood. It turned out that she had bleeding ulcers. She was thirteen at the time.

She went on to play tennis in college. But soon the stress was too great. She put down her racket at age nineteen and has not competed since. For five years, Rita and her father didn't talk to each other. Still, Rita says that her father is a brilliant coach, and that he loved his children and was dedicated to their success. Rita now lives in Las Vegas and teaches tennis.

Phillip played at the University of Nevada–Las Vegas, before giving up the game to help manage his brother Andre's vast business enterprises. Tami played at Texas A&M University, and is now a freelance sports promoter in Seattle. Though all three children were outstanding players, none had the talent to become a professional tennis player.

As for Andre, from the moment he was born, his father fixed on him as a future champion. Mike hung a tennis ball over baby Andre's crib when Betty brought him home from the hospital. A few days later, he put a little tennis racket in the baby's hand

and encouraged him to hit the hanging ball. "Even as a tiny baby he was able to follow with his eyes the flight of the ball through the air," Mike now remembers proudly. As soon as Andre was old enough to sit up, Mike tied a balloon to his high chair, and gave Andre a table-tennis racket to hit it with.

If Mike was fanatical about making his son a tennis star, Andre was equally passionate about tennis from the very start. At night, baby Andre insisted on sleeping with his tennis racket tucked in beside him.

When Andre was in a roll-around walker, Mike gave him a full-sized racket to hold. Andre began to hit glassware, salt shakers, and china cups. He broke them all, and many windows besides, before Betty Agassi removed the fragile objects from his reach.

As soon as Andre could walk, he started hitting tennis balls against the walls of his bedroom. Mike would stand on the other side of the closed door, smile, and nod his head. Andre had the drive and the talent to be a champion. He was sure of it.

Chapter Three
1972–1983

Prodigy and Troublemaker

By the time he was two and a half years old, Andre could serve overhand into a full-sized tennis court. He was so small that his father had to tape the racket to his hand so he could hold it. "He was born to play tennis," Mike said later. "He was born to be a great champion. I only gave him the mechanics, the desire, the will to win."

Andre certainly loved the game from the very beginning. Mike had to drag Andre off the tennis court every day when it was time to leave. While his brother and sisters hit seven thousand to eight thousand tennis balls a week, Andre would hit fourteen thousand. The specially rigged machines served 100-mile-per-hour bullets — with topspin and backspin, to the forehand and the backhand, serving up drop shots, lobs, and every kind of shot imaginable.

This was how Andre Agassi learned how to return serve. To this day, his service return is the best part of his tennis game. Many say it is the best, and most feared, service return in the world.

Mike also taught Andre many other secrets of the game. Because Andre was so small, he learned to hit his backhand two-fisted. Even now, this shot is one of his trademarks.

Mike Agassi also stressed the importance of getting the wrist into the shot. As the arm comes forward, the wrist has to stay back until the last moment, then flick forward, to give the racket extra force and speed as it hits the ball. This technique made Andre's shot faster and more powerful.

Mike Agassi believed in hitting every shot as hard as possible, and angling shots sharply. In short, he believed in thinking of every shot as a potential winner.

By the time little Andre was four years old, he was an emerging tennis prodigy. He played with his father's students and with visiting stars. On the courts of the Las Vegas hotels, he played practice rounds with champions Pancho Gonzales, Bobby Riggs, Ilie Nastase, Bjorn Borg, and Jimmy Connors.

All of them were very impressed with the tiny tennis whiz. "When he beats me," Connors joked with reporters, "I'll know it's time to retire." Andre later beat Connors several times — but Connors, another passionate lover of tennis, did not retire.

About the time Andre was five, his parents had saved up enough money to move to a bigger house. Almost as soon as they moved in, Mike began to build a tennis court in the backyard. He built it with his own sweat and with $21,000 of their hard-earned money. When it was done, he moved the ball machines he'd rigged up from the hotel courts to his own.

At age six, little Andre had already signed his first autograph. He discovered that he liked the attention he got when he played tennis. More important, he discovered his distinctive, winning style. He hit balls early, as his dad had taught him, just after they bounced and while they were still rising. This technique helped lend even more power to his strokes. He used an open stance and a furious snap of the wrist to give his forehand returns incredible torque.

By the time Andre was seven, he was playing in

tournaments. There weren't many important children's tennis events in Las Vegas. So every other weekend, Mike would pack the family into their station wagon and drive five hours to the California coast. When they got there, the family would all cram together into one room of a local motel. The next morning, playing with little sleep, the children would compete in the junior tournaments.

A man who, as a child, competed against Andre in his first under-ten tournament in Newport Beach remembers, "It was like being run over by an out-of-control, four-foot juggernaut." Andre, and all the Agassi children, played a brand of tennis that had never been seen among the more polite children of California.

Mike Agassi led the way. He would scream, curse, and complain to the officials from the sidelines. He would coach his kids during their matches, which was against the rules. He threatened people who argued with him, and would even get into fights with other kids' parents. Often, he had to be asked to leave the premises. His children, taking their cue from their father, were equally badly behaved, arguing with officials and displaying poor sportsmanship.

Today, the Agassi children defend Mike's actions. They feel he was right to complain; they say that the well-to-do tennis society of California did everything it could to make the matches extra hard for the outsiders, like scheduling their games first thing in the morning after the long drive from Las Vegas.

The Agassi children admit their father went overboard sometimes. (Jim Courier, a future rival of Andre's, remembers watching as a twelve-year-old when, after a junior tournament, Mike tossed Andre's third-place trophy in the trash.) But they say he did it because he loved his kids, and because he was on a short fuse after working two jobs to make ends meet. They point out that Mike Agassi always gave free tennis lessons to other children, because he loved them and he loved the game. Driven as he was, Mike Agassi had his tender side, too, his children insist.

One thing was for certain: his method produced winners. The Agassi children won most of their matches — especially Andre. He won his first nine matches in a row! Mike became obsessed with Andre's becoming number 1.

Andre, too, became obsessed, and soon tennis was

all he cared about. He didn't like school. One of his teachers said, "Andre has the attention span of a goldfish." Wherever Andre went, he carried a tennis racket with him. And wherever he went, the girl next door, Wendy Stewart, tagged along.

From the very beginning, when they were just toddlers, Wendy idolized Andre. When they were older, she was always ready to throw him tennis balls to hit, or just to watch him play. They would go swimming and skateboarding together, or just hang around talking. The two of them visited one another's houses, held hands as they sat on the sofa, watched TV, and ate junk food.

Perhaps what Andre liked most about pretty, dark-haired Wendy was her calm disposition. As fiery as he was, she was cool and levelheaded. Whenever he would get frustrated about school or about the long trips to California to play in tournaments, or even about the general unfairness of life, she would always try to calm him down.

Still, by the time he became a teenager, Andre Agassi was ready to explode. He was arguing with his father constantly, getting into fights, and doing poorly in school. "Why do I have to go to school?" he would complain. "I'm just wasting my time. There's nothing else I have to learn, anyway. I'm going to be a tennis player!"

Andre was headed down a dangerous road. By the age of twelve, he was hanging out with a gang of boys who liked getting into trouble just for the excitement. They weren't bad kids, really. But if they'd kept it up, they might have gone on to worse things.

One of Andre's pals from those days was Perry Rogers. Andre and Perry had met two years before, in a tournament for eleven-year-olds. Andre got beat very badly in an early-round match, and was going through one of his typical sore-loser tantrums. When Perry came up to him and tried to sympathize, Andre rudely told him to get lost. Perry didn't answer, but he did tell another boy how bad Andre's manners were. When word got back to Andre, he felt embarrassed at how he'd acted. He went to Perry and apologized. He also invited him to the movies. It was the beginning of a close friendship that has lasted for many years and is still going strong.

In those days, the two boys were always together. They would play hookey, and could often be found playing one-on-one basketball, soccer, or, of course, tennis. They went swimming together, saw movies together — and drank beer together. The two boys started hanging around with a much older crowd. They would go to a drive-in movie and get drunk, then go whoop it up and make mischief. They weren't violent, but, as Andre later put it, "I was falling down a deep hole."

Something had to change.

Something did.

Chapter Four
1984

The School of Hard Knocks

Mike Agassi had heard of Nick Bollettieri's Tennis Academy in Florida, but he didn't know much about it until one Sunday night when he happened to watch a report on *60 Minutes,* the CBS news program. The report focused on Bollettieri's iron discipline, the intense competition between the young players at the Academy, and the Academy's focus on producing future champions.

That was all Mike Agassi needed to hear. He had been looking for such a place for Andre. The iron discipline was just what his rebellious son needed. The intense competition against the best young players in the country would challenge Andre to work hard to improve his game. And Bollettieri's rigid focus on producing champions was like Mike Agassi's own. Mike felt confident about turning his son over to Bollettieri's guidance.

Mike asked around, seeking the advice of other local tennis coaches. They all agreed that if Andre stayed home, he would be a terrific tennis player but probably never world-class. With a challenging training program like Bollettieri's, though, he could be one of the best in the world.

Andre, too, wanted to go. Tennis was his life, it was what he loved the most. The idea of going to the Tennis Academy instead of a regular high school appealed to him. Maybe he could just forget about classes altogether, he fantasized. Or at least cut down on class time and homework. Anyway, it had to be better than what he was going through at home.

He and his dad were always at war. The rebellious Andre was doing outrageous things to get attention. His father refused to put up with his behavior and cracked down. Their battles carried onto the tennis courts as well. As much as Andre loved the game, if things went on like this between him and his dad much longer, he felt sure he would throw away his racket and tennis shoes and never go near a court again. Bollettieri's Academy sounded like a great escape to him.

There was only one problem: the Academy cost $2,800 a month! No way could the Agassis afford tuition like that. Still, Mike Agassi wasn't one to give in easily. He learned that Bollettieri, who was fanatic in his desire to produce a world champion, sometimes gave full scholarships to promising youngsters who otherwise couldn't afford his services. Mike was sure that Andre was good enough to get one of those scholarships.

And so, Mike and Andre flew the three thousand miles to Bradenton, Florida, to pay a visit to the Academy. Andre liked the look of the place: palm trees, sunny skies, pink stucco buildings, a beautiful swimming pool, lots of good-looking girls in cute tennis outfits.

Bollettieri liked the look of the thirteen-year-old Agassi, too: monster ground strokes, smashing service returns, a killer instinct. He quickly offered Andre a full scholarship. Mike Agassi rejoiced — his dreams for his son's future were coming true. The Agassis returned to Las Vegas to pack Andre's bags and to celebrate.

But as the time drew near for Andre to leave home, he began to have doubts about going. He was scared, although he would not have admitted it to anyone. He had never been away from home by himself before, let alone three thousand miles away! And in spite of the fact that he fought with his dad so much, Mike Agassi had been everything to Andre, the only coach he'd ever had. How would he get along with Nick Bollettieri? Would they hit it off?

Bollettieri had certainly seemed nice at first. He had a big, white-toothed smile, a perfect tan, and a bone-crushing handshake. He had produced Brian Gottfried, who had won a ton of tournaments and was then number 3 in the world. And he thought Andre could be number 1.

The night before he left, Andre's dad gave him $100 as a going-away present. Andre took the money, rented a chauffeur-driven stretch limousine, and went out for a night on the town with his best friend, Perry Rogers. That last night in Las Vegas, the two went to all their favorite haunts: Tramps, for southern-fried chicken fingers; Binion's, for burgers and fries; Mary's Diner, for strawberry milk shakes; and Ralph's Place, for double chocolate chip ice creams. Andre developed a taste for junk food at a very early age, and to this day, it's his favorite way to eat. Unfortunately, it has a nasty habit of adding pounds, and Andre has struggled now and then during his career to lose the extra weight he gains when he gives in to his appetite.

Andre didn't show his anxious feelings about going away until he got to Florida. Gone were his family and friends, the comforts of home, all the places and people he knew and loved. Suddenly, what had seemed a pretty cool place to spend the school year began to look like a prison.

The beautiful swimming pool, it turned out, was for the use of parents and visitors only. At Bollettieri's there was no time for partying or relaxing. Bollettieri, a former paratrooper, ran his Academy like a military school.

There were two uniformed security guards at the front gate, and they had German shepherds to help them patrol the fence. Wake-up time was 5:45 A.M. That was followed by a three-mile run on the beach, then cleanup of the dormitory, four hours of school, two and a half hours of tennis practice, then strenuous exercise, weight lifting, one and a half hours of homework, and finally, lights out at 10:30 P.M. The daily regimen of tennis consisted of hitting hundreds of balls a day, served up by faceless coaches or by dozens of machines. Weekends were for tournaments. Not a lot of time for fun.

Andre was instantly miserable, and furious that he'd been roped into coming here — forgetting that he'd been all for it himself. He was crammed into a small dormitory with seven other boys, one of whom was a tall young redhead, Jim Courier, who came from the tiny nearby town of Dade City. Jim was a quiet, polite boy, the very opposite of Andre.

Maybe it was because they came from such different backgrounds, or maybe it was because they were in competition with each other; whatever the reason, Courier and Agassi developed an instant dislike for each other, which still exists. Their rivalry is one of the greatest and most intense in all of tennis. Both have been number 1 in the world, and probably will be again.

Courier was not the only future champion at Bollettieri's back in 1983. Jimmy Arias and Aaron Krickstein were recent graduates, as was Carling Bassett. Those three were already making their mark on the professional tennis circuit. Curiously, all three would suffer burnout very quickly, perhaps as a result of their time at Bollettieri's. Of the three, only Krickstein recovered to continue his long, successful tennis career.

In a private cottage on the grounds lived young Monica Seles and her family. They had come all the way from Europe on a full scholarship — all their expenses paid by Bollettieri. David Wheaton and his family soon arrived from Minnesota, on a similar arrangement.

Bollettieri's training method consisted for the most part of finding the most promising young talent, nurturing their strengths, and ignoring their weaknesses. Most of Bollettieri's protégés featured big forehands and two-fisted backhands with a lot of topspin. As a rule, they weren't known for big serves and had weak volleying skills. They were aggressive, and for the most part they were winners.

Andre, at thirteen, hit the ball as well as any professional, so Nick Bollettieri soon focused on him as his prime contender for a future Grand Slam champion. That did not make Andre's schoolmates at the Academy very fond of him. Most of them were jealous, and many couldn't stand Andre's arrogant, rude attitude. As for Andre, he was as unhappy as he had ever been. He'd thought he would be getting away from his dad's harsh discipline, but Bollettieri's was even worse. He'd gone from the frying pan into the fire!

Chapter Five
1984-1986

Teen Terror

From the very beginning, Andre caused problems at the Academy. He would throw tantrums and break rackets every time he lost, which was often at first. He would break curfew and stay out late at night. He began to drink and to smoke marijuana — both of which he has since given up. (Andre is now one of the biggest anti-drug and anti-alcohol crusaders on the tennis tour.)

The rules at the Academy were very strict. There were regular room checks, and random checks with police dogs. A team of security guards was on constant patrol, twenty-four hours a day. Bollettieri was determined that there would be no forbidden activities at his Academy. But Andre Agassi was just as determined to defy the rules.

The school's code called for instant expulsion of

anyone caught breaking the rules. But Bollettieri didn't want to expel his star student, the one he planned to mold into his first Wimbledon champ. So Andre got away with things no one else could. That, in turn, convinced him he could do it again and again.

His on-court behavior wasn't much better than his off-court activities. He went through about forty Prince rackets a year, smashing them every time things didn't go his way. And for a while, things did not go well. Andre Agassi had been used to winning almost all the time. He was totally unaccustomed to losing 6–0, 6–0. Such losses upset Bollettieri, too, and he began to get impatient with his star pupil. Mike Agassi was even more upset. In their phone calls, he would scream at his son, urging him to straighten out and start winning.

The screaming, bullying, and iron discipline he was being subjected to didn't seem to tame Andre; instead, it made him even more rebellious. He would dress all in black so he could sneak out at night without being seen. Once on the prowl, he would commit small acts of vandalism, nothing too terrible, but enough to get him expelled if he was caught red-handed.

Some of the other students thought of Andre as a kind of hero. He was brave enough to rebel against the rules they hated but were too scared to do anything about. But most of the teens at the Academy thought of him as a spoiled brat — a maniac with bad manners, a wicked temper, and a big self-destructive streak.

Even Andre Agassi himself, looking back on those days, realizes his behavior was way out of bounds. "You know, they're right. I was just so obnoxious," he says now. "I was a real head-case. I was just so lonely; no one will ever know how lonely. . . ."

He began to dress outrageously and wear weird hairdos. Every month, it would be something different, as if he were saying "Pay attention to me!" with every move he made. He went from a shaved head, to a Hare Krishna (a bald head with a ponytail on top), to a Mohawk. That was too much for the principal of the regular school the Academy's students attended. He told Andre to stop acting up or he'd risk expulsion. That was all Andre needed to hear. The next day, he showed up with his Mohawk dyed platinum blond!

By Christmas 1985, he had been at the Academy

more than two years, and was going out of his mind with frustration. A Mohawk hairdo was no longer enough. Andre decided to give himself something really weird for Christmas. He arrived at the airport in Las Vegas for Christmas vacation with his hair in punk-style spikes and dyed in multicolored stripes! His father nearly had a stroke. Everyone in Las Vegas, a place where they see just about everything, was shocked.

When he got back to the Academy, he came close to getting kicked out. But Bollettieri held his fire. He sensed that Andre's fiery temperament, his creativity and originality — which were being expressed in crazy, self-destructive ways — could be channeled into his playing. In fact, thought Bollettieri, they might just be the seeds of Andre's future success. He was a rebel. "Kill that off," Bollettieri later commented, "and I might have killed off the champion inside him."

By this time, Andre had turned his game around and was whipping his teenage competition left and right. Even so, things could not go on as they had for much longer. During a tournament in Pensacola, Florida, Andre was playing the best tennis of his life, winning with ease in round after round. Then he showed up for the final wearing ripped jeans, an earring, pink lipstick, and eyeliner. The crowd, ready to cheer his entrance, was shocked and silent. Bollettieri was steaming. He called Andre out in front of everybody at the Academy and publicly humiliated him. Andre took it all without a word in reply. He simply turned, walked back to his dorm, and packed his bags. Next thing anyone knew, he was through the front gates, walking toward the airport — thirty miles away.

Bollettieri didn't rush after him. He had seen plenty of teen tantrums before. Besides, Andre had no money or credit cards. Those were in Bollettieri's safekeeping. He would give Andre a good two-hour head start. Plenty of time to think things out and cool down. Then, and only then, did he go after him.

They spent more than two hours that day in Bollettieri's office, airing all their complaints with each other. Bollettieri was impressed with the depth of Andre's feelings, and by how sincerely he expressed them. He decided to give his star pupil another chance.

Nothing changed at first. Andre had discovered

that the madder he got, the better he played, so the on-court tantrums continued. But the student and the teacher had forged a deeper bond, one that would cause trouble for Bollettieri soon enough, as some of his other talented students grew jealous of the time, energy, and attention he lavished on Agassi.

Bollettieri had decided that what Andre needed was to play against better, more experienced opponents. Just after his sixteenth birthday, at Bollettieri's urging, Andre turned professional. It was May 1, 1986 — the beginning of a wild ride, an illustrious career with dizzying highs and desperate lows. And although he continued to act like a child for a very long time after, it was the end of Andre Agassi's childhood.

Chapter Six
1986–1987
The Young Professional

Andre had high hopes that by turning professional he would escape from the Academy in Bradenton. He hated it in Florida, so far from home, from Perry, Wendy, and his other close friends. Only by winning, he knew, could he convince his dad that it was okay for him to leave school altogether and just be a tennis player.

Being a pro on the junior circuit meant a lot of traveling apart from the regular Bollettieri crew. So Andre's older brother, Phillip, agreed to accompany him on his travels. Phil went everywhere with Andre. He slept on the hotel-room floor, made all the arrangements, made sure Andre's rackets were in good tournament shape, even planned their meals. "I've heard that Andre missed his childhood," Phil has said since. "I did, too."

Though Andre did manage to get away from the Academy and its marine-corps discipline for part of the year, he was still unhappy. All the hairdos and weird dressing up were just a disguise, something to hide the scared Andre, who was hurting inside. He figured that if he looked cool, he would *be* cool.

But if he had escaped his father's yelling and Bollettieri's scolding, he could not escape the fans. They were impressed with his tennis all right, but they were horrified by his manners on the court. Andre argued with the officials, screamed at them, bullied them. He hit easy winning shots right at his opponents' faces or stomachs instead of into the empty court. He smashed his rackets and stormed off the court if he was losing, or if calls went against him.

In his very first professional match, against a man named Marko Ostoja, he argued with the referee so much that Ostoja eventually joined in. "Why don't you just shut up and stay out of it!" Agassi roared at his opponent. At which point, Ostoja, who had a reputation as a "bad boy" himself, reached out and smacked Andre hard across the face.

It seemed that Andre was uneasy wherever he was.

Whenever he managed to get home, he saw Perry, Wendy, and the others having a great time, partying around town and enjoying one another's company. It made him feel even worse. So when he came home for the Las Vegas Open, he took his pain and anger out on the court with him.

He behaved so badly that the crowd began rooting against the hometown boy. In fact, Andre didn't even want to be there. He had been in big tournaments five weeks in a row, and only entered this one because Phil begged him. Andre's older brother, while not good enough to go professional on his own, wanted to play doubles with Andre as a team. After all Phil was doing for him, Andre couldn't refuse. But he didn't have to like being there.

People in the stands began booing him whenever he cursed at the referee or at an opponent. "Shut up!" he finally exploded, screaming at the fans and throwing his racket. It was just as bad as being yelled at by his dad or Bollettieri, Andre felt. Pretty soon, Andre Agassi was being called "the bad boy of tennis." He was extremely unhappy, but he couldn't seem to change his ways. He continued to take out his anger on his opponents.

Only eighty-nine days into his professional career, and ninety-one days after his sixteenth birthday, Andre found himself in his first pro final match, against Ramesh Krishnan in the prestigious Challenger Tournament in Schenectady, New York. Krishnan had been a professional for eight years, was number 1 in India, and had made the Wimbledon quarterfinals just a few weeks before.

Krishnan ended Andre's pursuit of his first pro title. But Andre had made people sit up and take notice. Though his manners were horrifying, his playing continued to impress. He reached two semifinals that first season, raising his world ranking from 681 to 91 in just a few short months.

At that time, the men's tennis world was looking for a new star. The great players who had lots of charisma — Bjorn Borg, Arthur Ashe, Ken Rosewall, Adriano Panatta, Manuel Orantes — had mostly all retired. Jimmy Connors and John McEnroe still livened up the circuit, but they, too, were getting old in tennis terms. The top players in 1986 were less flashy, particularly the Americans.

The Europeans had Boris Becker and Yannick Noah. But the millions of American fans who had flocked to tennis in the days of Chris Evert and Jimmy Connors had grown bored. They were now turning away from tennis, tired of the dull play and the lack of interesting personalities. Where was the rising star wrapped in charisma and glamour?

It was at that precise moment that Andre Agassi burst upon the scene, with his flashy dress, his weird haircuts, his startling talent, and his in-your-face attitude. People began to take notice of this sixteen-year-old firebrand.

The Challenger Series had gone well, but by 1987, Andre Agassi had bigger fish to fry. He made his first trip abroad for the Seoul Open in Korea in April of that year. In that event, he reached the final, where he lost in a close, well-contested match.

Feeling the power of his game and the thrill of realizing that he could play against seasoned professionals and win, Andre arrived in London that June for his first Wimbledon tournament. He passed through the gates of the All England Club, where his father had once stood, watching the limousines pass through. Mike Agassi had dreamed that someday he would play here, would win here. He never did, but now, his son Andre had made it.

The Wimbledon championship is one of the four top annual events in tennis. Called Grand Slams, they also include the French Open, the Australian Open, and the U.S. Open.

The French Open is played on the slow clay surface of Roland Garros Stadium, and it favors baseliners, players who stay back and pound out returns, never coming to the net. The U.S. and Australian Opens are played on hard courts, made of man-made, composite materials, which are much faster than clay. Here, serve-and-volleyers, players who smash out big serves and come straight up to the net, do better.

Wimbledon, however, is the fastest kind of court of all. It is made of grass and has an uneven surface. A baseliner is at a big disadvantage there. Such a player was Andre Agassi. With all his confidence, he was not prepared for the speed of the courts, or for the strength of the competition. In the second round, he was unceremoniously bounced by Henri Leconte of France, 6–2, 6–1, 6–2.

Leconte was playing in his sixth Wimbledon. He had reached the semifinals the year before, and the quarterfinals the year before that. Andre looked and felt like a beginner playing against him on the unfamiliar, unforgiving grass of Wimbledon. He was devastated by the defeat. He shouldn't have been. After all, losses are a part of tennis, even for the best players. And Andre was playing against the best in the whole world, not the best of the junior circuit, as before. Still, the defeat stung him badly. It would be many years before he would return to Wimbledon.

For a player of his talents, Andre Agassi was incredibly insecure. Every time he played badly, he would fall into despair over his future. After one particular 1987 loss in a tournament in Washington, D.C., he went across the street to a public park, and with tears in his eyes, gave all his rackets away to two old men playing checkers.

Why was Andre so insecure? His old friend Perry Rogers feels it was because Andre didn't have a real childhood, or any identity besides being a tennis player. He was afraid that if he failed at tennis, he wouldn't be anybody at all.

That summer, he was back at the Academy, moping over his Wimbledon loss and feeling generally miserable about his life. He had become a professional tennis player, sure, but he had totally missed his childhood to get there.

One day at the Academy, he fell into conversation with Mary Jane Wheaton, the mother of David Wheaton, a schoolmate. Mary Jane was a very religious woman. She asked him where he thought he would go when he died. Andre told her he didn't know. In spite of the fact that his parents had taken the kids to church when they were little, Andre had never been religious. He had gotten into many things, most of them bad. But he had never really thought about God.

He began to spend time with Fritz Glauss, the traveling vicar on the tennis circuit. The other players would be in the locker room, talking about girls and parties and money, while Andre and Glauss sat there talking about heaven, and doing unto others as you would have them do unto you.

With Glauss, Mary Jane and David Wheaton, young Michael Chang, who was also at the Academy, and others, Andre began to attend group Bible discussions and prayer meetings. When he returned to Las Vegas for visits, he attended the Meadows Fellowship Church. The pastor there, John Parenti, was just as wild a dresser as Andre, so the young tennis prodigy felt right at home.

At first, Andre had been afraid that by becoming more in tune with his religion, he would have to tame himself, and that it would destroy his aggressive tennis game. But in the end, he realized that he could continue to be himself and still be a deeply religious person. Andre insists that it was his discovery of God that turned his life around then. He started accepting a lot of the criticism he'd been rejecting from those around him. More important, he began to deal with the enormous pressures of his life.

Andre never talks much about his religious beliefs, but ever since that day in 1987, they have been a constant part of his life. He says they changed the way he approached his tennis game, and judging from the results, he's probably right.

Putting the Wimbledon disaster behind him, Andre went on to have a fantastic year playing on friendlier surfaces. At the Basle Indoor in Switzerland, he reached the semifinals before losing to Yannick Noah. And at Stratton Mountain, Vermont, he made it to the semifinals again, where he proceeded to give John McEnroe a run for his money. After squeezing out a victory, McEnroe said, "I've never played against anyone who hit the ball so hard, so often, and so accurately."

Then, in November, the seventeen-year-old boy wonder arrived in Itaparica, Brazil, for the South American Open. The S.A. Open is a very prestigious tournament with a huge first prize, a Grand Prix event ranked just below the four Grand Slam events. Andre surprised everyone by winning the tournament!

By year's end, he had gone from number 91 in the world to number 25. Now, everyone was watching him. He was no longer a potential star — Andre Agassi was the real thing.

Chapter Seven
1988

Rising Star

In 1987, Andre really arrived on the men's tennis scene. But as good a year as he had, no one could have predicted what was about to happen in 1988.

In fact, the year started out badly for Andre. In mid-February, he ran up against Miloslav Mecir of Slovakia, in a tournament in Amsterdam, the Netherlands. Mecir was a brilliant player, but he was inconsistent. On this particular day, though, he was on top of his game, and he worked his magic on Agassi, making Andre look like a complete amateur.

A year earlier, Andre might have let a defeat like this get to him. But now, with his newfound faith and his stronger sense of himself as a person, not just a tennis player, Andre was quick to turn things around.

The very next week, on February 21, he won his second Grand Prix title, the U.S. National Indoor

Championship in Memphis, Tennessee. His opponent in that final was Mikael Pernfors of Sweden, a player nearly as flamboyant as Andre. Pernfors was well known for wearing his hair in wild styles — once he even dyed it to resemble the blue-and-yellow Swedish flag.

Pernfors was not just a showman, though; he'd recently been ranked in the top 10, and had beaten both Henri Leconte (the man who'd obliterated Andre at Wimbledon) and Boris Becker. So when Andre stepped onto the court, blond ponytail and all, few people thought he could handle Pernfors.

But on this day, Andre Agassi showed his true talent — and a newfound politeness that surprised even those who knew him best. He joked with the officials, congratulated Pernfors whenever he made a great shot, and even cracked jokes for the crowd. When Pernfors cursed at himself in Swedish for missing a shot, Andre piped up: "That's easy for you to say, Mikael." The crowd roared with laughter.

Andre was being lovable, and the crowd fell in love with him. When he won the match with one final, two-fisted backhand smash, he ran to the stands to hug his family, then gave his racket to a young fan in a wheelchair. The newspapers spread the picture all over the next day's sports pages.

Tennis fans in America and around the world had found themselves a new hero. He was charismatic, charming, good-natured, polite, and an incredible player. His name was Andre Agassi.

Those who had been put off by Andre's past behavior shook their heads. This hero image was nothing like the spoiled teenager they knew. They were sure it could not last. As soon as people got to see the real Andre, the bubble would burst, they were sure of it.

But for the moment, it seemed, nothing could stop Andre Agassi's rise to the top. Nick Bollettieri began traveling around the world to be at his protégé's side for all his major tournaments, which angered many of his other students, particularly Jim Courier and Monica Seles, both of whom broke with Bollettieri because of it. Neither wanted to be a second-class citizen. To this day, they are bitter at what they see as their ex-mentor's favoritism.

But Bollettieri believed that Andre Agassi was his ticket to fame, his future number 1. So, when Andre reached the final of the U.S. Clay Court Championship in Charleston, South Carolina, on May 1 of that year, Bollettieri was there in the courtside box with the Agassi family.

Andre's opponent in that match was none other than Jimmy Arias, another of Bollettieri's one-time superstars. Arias had suffered burnout from the intense pressure of being a teenage phenomenon, but he was making a comeback on the circuit. Andre Agassi soon put a stop to that by beating Arias.

Only a week later, Andre added yet another title to his growing collection, with a victory over Slobodan Zivojinovic of Yugoslavia, in the Tournament of Champions in Forest Hills, New York. Zivojinovic had been in or near the top 20 for a long time, but Andre was equal to his best efforts.

It was around this time that Andre played his first match as a member of America's Davis Cup team. The Davis Cup is the World Series of tennis, in which teams from different countries compete for the World Championship. Contests between countries consist of five matches — four singles and one doubles — which together are called "ties." The winner of the most matches (at least three out of five) in a given tie advances to the next round.

Andre's first tie was a semifinal round against Peru,

in Lima, that country's capital. There, he beat home-town hero Jaime Yzaga, 6–8, 7–5, 6–1, 6–2. For Agassi, who went on to play in the final, it was the beginning of a long, illustrious Davis Cup career.

By the time the Italian Open rolled around later that month, everyone in the tennis world had their eyes on the "Blond Bomber" from America. The Italian Open is a raucous tournament, with pas-sionate fans who think nothing of screaming for their hero as he walks out onto the court. Beauti-ful men and women parade around in the latest ten-nis fashions, and charisma counts for as much as talent.

No wonder then, that Andre Agassi made a big splash when he turned up that May in Rome. Girls swooned when he came onto the court; they screamed when he took off his shirt at the end of a winning match and threw it into the crowd. Andre was their new idol, and he played well besides, giv-ing the adoring crowd their money's worth. He made it all the way to the semifinals before losing a close match to Guillermo Perez-Roldan of Argentina, who had been French Open Junior Champion the previ-ous two years. Perez-Roldan went on to lose in the final to Ivan Lendl of Czechoslovakia, number 1 in the world at that time.

Next up for Andre was the French Open, the most important clay court event of the year in tennis. Clay court tennis is as different from the grass court game as softball is from baseball. On clay, where you have more time to react, rallies can last more than a hundred shots, and matches sometimes go on for five hours and more. On grass the ball comes at you more quickly and volleys rarely last long, and an overpowering serve is all but unbeatable.

Andre Agassi went to Roland Garros Stadium ready to play and full of confidence. In the fourth round, he defeated Magnus Gustafsson of Sweden, and then found himself face to face with Perez-Roldan in the quarterfinals — the very man who had beaten him in Rome two weeks earlier. This time, Andre was ready for him and primed for revenge. He obliterated the Argentine and stormed into the semifinals.

There, he was paired with the great Mats Wilander of Sweden, who had won the French Open twice and reached the final two other times, including the year before. Wilander had won five Grand Slam titles, including victories on all three types of court. No one thought the young American had a chance.

But Andre gave Wilander the fight of his life in a classic tennis match that day in May 1988. Wilander pulled it out in five sets, 4–6, 6–2, 7–5, 5–7, 6–0. After placing his shots perfectly for four sets, hitting the line an incredible number of times, Andre finally tired, mentally and physically, in the last set.

Afterward, Wilander told reporters that if anyone doubted whether Agassi had the game and the mind to be a champion, they could put those doubts to rest. "No matter how hard he hits the ball, he hits it with amazing accuracy," Wilander said.

The next month, it came as a great surprise to the tennis world when Andre announced that he planned to skip Wimbledon that year. Rumors immediately began: Andre was running scared, his handlers were trying to protect him from another depressing defeat on grass. People shook their heads in dismay and disappointment. Andre had risen from number 89 to number 5 in the world in just five months. And yet, he was refusing to play in the world's number one tournament, the tournament that has always defined great champions.

Was Andre scared? Through his agent, Bill Shelton, he said he was "tired." Yet he continued to play in tournaments for the next four months without taking a week off. At about the time Stefan Edberg was defeating Boris Becker for his first Wimbledon title, Andre and John McEnroe went to Buenos Aires for a Davis Cup tie against home-team Argentina, led by Guillermo Perez-Roldan and Martin Jaite.

The Argentines were almost unbeatable at home, having defeated the Americans (and McEnroe) the last four times they'd played there. McEnroe was out for revenge, and Agassi helped him get it. While McEnroe handled Perez-Roldan, Agassi made mincemeat of Jaite on clay, the Argentine's favorite surface, 6–2, 6–2, 6–1. McEnroe was amazed, telling anyone who would listen that Agassi had what it took to be a champion.

In the next few months, Agassi went on an incredible streak, winning twenty-three matches in a row. He won the Mercedes Cup in Stuttgart, Germany, the Volvo International at Stratton Mountain, Vermont, and the Mennen Cup in Illinois — all three Grand Prix events. The Grand Prix circuit is just one step below the Grand Slam, and the events are all hot contests.

Then came September, and the U.S. Open, in Flushing Meadow, New York. Andre Agassi arrived as the new heartthrob of the tennis world, as the new American hero. Young, handsome, stylish, devil-may-care, and rebellious, he was the son of poor immigrants, he read the Bible every day, and he was an underdog in this tournament. He had lost in the first round here the previous two years, but now, many people, including Andre himself, believed he could beat the odds and win.

Andre breezed through the first four rounds, including a fourth-round victory over sixteen-year-old rising star Michael Chang. Then, in the quarterfinals, he came up against a legend.

Jimmy Connors had himself once been dubbed "the bad boy of tennis." For years, the "Brash Basher" had sliced up opponents with his fierce play, and won devoted fans with his magnetic personality. Connors was thirty-six years old now — considered to be long past his prime — but he was still out there playing, and he had chosen the U.S. Open that year to stage a comeback. Connors was playing such wonderful tennis that his fans thought he could actually go all the way.

Before the match, Bollettieri took Andre aside and warned him not to take the aging champion lightly. Connors had won the U.S. Open five times, Wimbledon twice, and the Australian Open once. But Andre was so sure of his own abilities, so confident in his game, that he thought he could dispatch Connors easily. He was right.

In the match, Andre played some of the best tennis of his life, a magnificent, nearly error-free display. He never gave Connors an opening, defeating him easily, 6–2, 7–6, 6–1. The thousands of fans in the stands and the millions watching around the world on TV were stunned. This eighteen-year-old newcomer was amazing!

Andre wound up being eliminated in the semifinals, but he had established himself as a likely future champion. For him, 1988 had been a breakthrough year. He had won six Grand Prix titles out of the seven finals he made. Three of those titles had been on hard courts, and three on clay, proving he could master both surfaces. He had made it to the semifinals in the two Grand Slam events he'd entered, the French and the U.S. Opens. He had reached the quarterfinals in thirteen of the sixteen tournaments he'd competed in. He had had winning streaks of twenty-three matches and thirteen matches. He had a Davis Cup record of three wins and no losses in his first year of competition. He had made it to number 3 in the world. And last but not least, he had earned more than $2 million in prize money.

"Even now," Andre said much later, "I sometimes look back at that year and think, Phew, did I really do that?"

Chapter Eight
1989

The Slump

Although it seemed as if nothing could stop the meteoric rise of Andre Agassi, there was trouble brewing. Andre had shown the world he could play with the best of them — but he had also shown the world another side of himself.

His actions on the court when he was losing a match were well known: his tendency to deliberately give up on a set when he was behind, saving his energy for the next set. He had done this to John McEnroe during their 1988 Volvo Cup match, and McEnroe had become furious. "It's insulting, immature, and a copout," he complained to reporters later.

Though he had his lovable moments, Andre's penchant for arguing with referees and linesmen, insulting opponents and fans, using foul language, and smashing rackets was still infuriating to many people.

But his actions as a winner had made him even more enemies on the tennis circuit. Whenever he was way ahead in a match, he would exaggerate being a good sport, applauding especially good shots his opponents made and correcting the linesmen when they made wrong calls in his favor. Most people in the crowd liked Andre for this, but his opponents saw it as rubbing it in.

For instance, during the Davis Cup match with Argentina, Andre actually turned to Bollettieri in the stands, said, "Watch this, Nick," and caught one of his opponent's shots in his hand! The crowd booed him, and his opponent, Martin Jaite, was outraged. He felt that Andre was humiliating him on purpose.

Andre's dashing good looks had won him many female fans. His on-court antics — bowing to the crowd whenever they applauded, pretending to bribe the linesmen, cheering for himself, blowing kisses, and throwing his shirts into the stands — made him great entertainment. This was not lost on the business world. Companies began to come after Andre, offering him big money to endorse their products.

In the 1990 French Open, Andre Agassi hits a crushing forehand against fellow American Jim Courier, whom he later defeated, 6–7, 6–1, 6–0.

Agassi's powerful serve helped him defeat Germany's Boris Becker during the men's singles quarterfinals at Wimbledon in 1992.

Overcome with emotion, Andre Agassi accepts the 1992 Wimbledon trophy from the Duke of Kent. Agassi defeated Goran Ivanisevic in the best-of-five final, 6–7, 6–4, 6–4, 1–6, 6–4.

A smashing backhand return rockets off the racket of Agassi to opponent Thomas Muster of Austria during the U.S. Open in 1994.

The winner of the 1994 U.S. Open celebrates! Agassi defeated Germany's Michael Stich, 6–1, 7–6, 7–5.

"If I can make a positive impact on at least one child's life, then it has all been worthwhile." —Andre Agassi, after donating $1 million to the Las Vegas Boys and Girls Club.

Agassi celebrates a victory over Pete Sampras, 3–6, 6–2, 7–6 (7–3) in the Lipton Championships in 1995.

AP/Wide World Photos

Now the number 1 seeded player in the world, Agassi gives it his all in a match against Patrick McEnroe at Wimbledon in 1995.

Reaching high, Agassi sends the ball over the net to Alex Corretja of Spain in the 1995 U.S. Open.

Tired but victorious, Andre Agassi takes a moment to mop his brow.

A special moment shared between Andre Agassi and his fiancée, actress Brooke Shields.

Andre Agassi's Career Highlights

1988:
Semifinalist, French Open
Semifinalist, U.S. Open

1989:
Semifinalist, U.S. Open

1990:
Member of champion Davis Cup team
Finalist, French Open
Finalist, U.S. Open

1991:
Winner, ATP World Championship
Finalist, French Open

1992:
Winner, Wimbledon men's singles championship

1994:
Winner, U.S. Open

1995:
Winner, Australian Open
Winner, Canadian Open
Finalist, U.S. Open
Semifinalist, Wimbledon men's singles championship

1996:
Olympic gold medalist, men's singles
Semifinalist, U.S. Open

Andre began to sign deals that made him more money than he could make on the tennis court. His face appeared on billboards and in magazine ads, and he appeared in numerous TV commercials. He was everywhere, which only made him more popular with the fans — and less popular with his fellow tennis players. Perhaps they were jealous. Few of them were as sought-after by the media or advertisers. To them, it must have seemed as if Andre was being rewarded for behaving badly.

There was a lot of ill-will toward Andre floating around the tennis tour. As long as he was winning, the whispering and criticism didn't bother him. But as veteran player Ion Tiriac commented, "God help Agassi if and when he starts losing."

Nineteen eighty-nine began with Andre deciding for the third year in a row not to play in the Australian Open. That was upsetting to players and fans alike. After all, they thought, he is the number 3 player in the world. Why won't he play in one of the four biggest tournaments of the season?

Instead of going to Australia, Andre took a long vacation in Las Vegas. Then he was off to Fort Myers, Florida, for a Davis Cup match against Paraguay.

The last time the two countries had met, in Asunción, Paraguay's capital, the Americans had been beaten. Now they were out for revenge. Andre was whipping his singles opponent when, in the third set, he began taunting him. "It was time to rub it in," he said later, explaining his unforgivable outburst. "But I wasn't making fun of him. I was making fun of Paraguay." To many people, attempting to show patriotism by ridiculing another country was just another example of Andre's unacceptable on-court behavior.

Andre's next move was in the world of business. He signed a $6 million deal with Donnay, the Belgian tennis racket company. Never mind that Andre had been playing with (and destroying) Prince rackets since he was a toddler. Six million was six million!

There was only one problem. Andre soon found that he could not play as well with his new, designer rackets. At the Newsweek Championship in Indian Wells, California, he was spotted using a Prince racket with a big "D" (the Donnay logo) painted on the strings! His agent denied it, and eventually Andre did get used to his new rackets, but his tennis game suffered for a while.

Things were changing in his private life as well. At that year's Volvo International (an event he'd won the year before), Andre broke up with his longtime girlfriend, Wendy Stewart, dropping her for Amy Moss, a student from Tennessee who was working as a volunteer driver for the players. Amy was a devout Christian, like Andre, and she was also a beautiful blonde. Wendy went home to Las Vegas, crushed. She still loved Andre, and in her heart she believed he'd come back to her. Two years later, he did.

For the moment, Amy and Andre were a hot item on the tennis circuit. The two loved to dress up and go out late at night to parties and dance clubs, where they would hang out with other celebrities.

Wherever Andre went, Amy went with him. So did his brother, Phil; Nick Bollettieri, now his coach; Bill Shelton; Fritz Glauss; his trainer Gil Reyes; and people from Donnay, Nike, and the other companies whose products Andre was now representing.

With his off-court life so busy, it was perhaps no surprise that his game took a dive in early 1989. He was bounced in the first round of the Lipton International in Key Biscayne, Florida, by Carl-Uwe

Steeb of Germany. Fellow Bollettieri protégé David Wheaton blew Andre out of another tournament.

By the time the Italian Open came around that May, Andre had slid down in the rankings and was in a foul temper most of the time. But his nineteenth birthday, and the trip to Rome, where he'd been so well received the year before, seemed to inspire Andre. He played so well that he reached the final. It was the best he'd done in six months.

Then, in the final, he was beaten by Alberto Mancini of Argentina in five sets, 3–6, 6–4, 6–2, 6–7, 1–6. Andre was so upset that he screamed at Phil in front of reporters and cameramen.

The French Open was another disaster for Andre. He went down in the third round, in straight sets, to none other than Jim Courier, his old rival from the Academy. Even worse, the tournament was ultimately won by seventeen-year-old Michael Chang, Andre's Bible-reading partner.

Chang had no power at all in his serve. It was practically underhand. He wasn't very fast, either. His game, as honed by Bollettieri, relied on perfectly placed shots and outlasting his opponents with his superior stamina. Younger than Agassi, seeded 14th in the tournament, and without much of a power game, Chang had won with a combination of finesse and endurance — to become the youngest-ever winner of a Grand Slam event. It was Chang, not Agassi, who was now America's rising star.

Wimbledon was only two weeks away. Once again, for the second year in a row, Andre decided not to enter the world's greatest tournament. Now the grumbling was out in the open. Andre was afraid, people said: He was ducking competition with the world's best players, afraid he would lose badly. He was trying to keep his ranking high by playing only against players he could beat.

Andre's excuse was that he was tired and needed to rest for a few weeks. But that didn't change the truth: he had gotten to number 3 in the world without ever playing against seven of the other top 10 players.

In September, the U.S. Open rolled around again. As had happened the year before, Andre found himself in a quarterfinal matchup against the great Jimmy Connors, now one year older and in the middle of an even more successful run for the title.

Many expected Connors to get revenge this time.

Andre had looked very beatable all year long. But Agassi put a great match together and beat Connors in a five-set marathon, 6–1, 4–6, 0–6, 6–3, 6–4. Yet what impressed his fans was that it was the first time Andre had come from behind to win a five-set match in professional competition.

Throughout his career, Andre had had a reputation for giving up as soon as he started to lose. But that day, he'd come back from a deficit of two sets to one. Even though he lost in the semifinals again, he had proved that he still had the ability to persevere and come out a winner.

But no sooner did he show that ability than once again he faced criticism for giving in to his old ways. In the final of the World Championship of Tennis Cup in Dallas, Andre was losing 0–3 to John McEnroe in the second set (after winning the first). Suddenly, he walked off the court limping, forfeiting the match because of "a pulled muscle." Although no one but Andre can say how serious the injury was, some thought he should not have given up the match. In fact, one observer called it "a disgraceful surrender."

Then, when shortly afterward McEnroe went

down with his own injury, Agassi came to the Davis Cup team's rescue. He beat Henri Leconte, who had beaten him at Wimbledon two years earlier, in four sets, 6–1, 6–2, 6–7, 6–1. Then he took on Yannick Noah and beat him in straight sets to help the United States to a 5–0 victory.

The win over France propelled the U.S. team into a semifinal tie with West Germany. Andre found himself paired against Boris Becker. The two played a steamy five-set match. Andre won the first two sets on tie-breakers and was leading 6–5 in the third set, just one game away from winning, when the tide turned. Becker, in front of his countrymen, held his serve, and then won the tie-break to earn back a set. That put him on a roll. The German won the fourth set to even things up, just as darkness fell. The fifth and last set had to be postponed until the next day. When play resumed, Becker finally won, 6–4.

Agassi then lost his second match as well, to Carl-Uwe Steeb, 6–4, 4–6, 4–6, 2–6. Again, as soon as he was behind in the match, Agassi's play went downhill, as if he had given up at the first sign of trouble.

What was wrong with Andre? Was he just going through a rough period following his incredible 1988 season? Or was it part of his personality to give up when things went wrong?

Andre finally won a title that October, when he was victorious over Brad Gilbert in the final of the Orlando Classic in Florida. But in his final tournament of the year, the Grand Prix Masters at Madison Square Garden in New York, he played poorly from the very beginning on opening night, losing his first round-robin match to Stefan Edberg of Sweden, 4–6, 2–6. He then proceeded to lose to Boris Becker and Brad Gilbert, to end the tournament at 0 and 3.

Andre Agassi finished 1989 with winnings totalling less than half his 1988 earnings. With all his endorsement contracts, he was still making millions, but it didn't erase the sting of having played so badly all season long. He went home to Las Vegas for Christmas, depressed and discouraged.

Chapter Nine
1990–1992

Revival

The year 1990 began the way the previous three had, with Andre deciding to skip the Australian Open. At this point, no one was surprised. Clearly, young Agassi was having trouble putting his life — and his tennis game — in order.

He quit the Davis Cup team when coach Tom Gorman insisted that he bring only one guest with him to Carlsbad, California, to play the Mexican team.

Then, as if the fight with Gorman had awoken him from a long sleep, Agassi went on to win the Volvo Classic in San Francisco, the first event on the new ATP tour. He followed that victory up with another in March at the Newsweek Cup in Indian Wells, California.

But win or lose, Andre Agassi had become a very

well known sports figure. Nike was making him a media star, providing him with ultrawild tennis outfits to wear on the court (including an orange-and-black "hot lava" ensemble), and featuring him on huge billboards all across the country, with slogans like "Just Do It" and "The Hair Apparent." One of his ad campaigns, for Canon cameras, became famous for the slogan "Image Is Everything." The words became identified with Andre, and still are.

Always flashy in appearance, Andre stopped shaving, started wearing an earring in one ear, and painted his pinky fingernail. His daring new look seemed to be matched by his play, as he went on to win the Lipton International Players Championship by beating the number 1 player in the world, Stefan Edberg, in the final.

Edberg was amazed at the quality of Andre's tennis. He and Andre became friends, and they have a mutual respect for each other's talent that survives to this day. On that day, Andre was the better player. "Andre is good for tennis," Edberg said. "It would be pretty boring if tennis was populated by hordes of Stefan Edbergs."

Though he was gaining the respect of his fellow

players, Andre continued to excite controversy in the world of tennis. The head of the French Open, offended by Andre's fashion statements, threatened to institute an "all-white" dress code, like at Wimbledon. But Andre stood his ground, saying that he would go home to Las Vegas if that happened. The French Open was just another tournament, as far as he was concerned. Of course he didn't mean it, but the head of the Open backed down, and Andre appeared in full costume for his opening-round match.

Spectators at the French Open saw Andre play some superb tennis, but they also witnessed his bad behavior. He lost the first set of his opening-round match to Canadian Martin Wolstenholme, ranked 122 in the world, before beating him in four sets. During that match, Andre, in a fit of temper, cursed at the umpire and commanded him to come down out of his chair to check out a ball mark on the court. Andre also smashed an easy winner right at Wolstenholme, hitting him. He didn't apologize, either. The crowd was horrified.

Though he was fined for his outburst, Andre refused to temper himself. He continued to play great tennis, mowing down his old rival Jim Courier in the fourth round, beating defending champion Michael Chang in the quarterfinals, and outlasting Sweden's Jonas Svensson in a four-set semifinal match.

That put Andre into his first Grand Slam final, against Ecuador's Andres Gomez. After Andre's temper tantrums, the crowd was rooting for Gomez. He made them happy by beating Andre, 6–3, 2–6, 6–4, 6–4, with a display of finesse so dazzling that it overwhelmed Andre's power game.

Andre was stunned — he could not believe he had lost. Even more upset was Nick Bollettieri, who, from his seat in the stands, had been assuring everyone who would listen that this was the day he'd been waiting thirty years for, the day one of his pupils won a Grand Slam event.

After his humiliating defeat, Andre announced that he was skipping Wimbledon yet again. He went home and spent five weeks in Las Vegas recovering his spirit and his physical strength, working out daily with trainer Gil Reyes.

By late July, he was back in action. He won a tournament in Washington, D.C., then lost badly over the next three weeks to Michael Chang, Richard Fromberg of Australia, and Peter Lundgren of Sweden, all of whom were ranked below him. He complained that he couldn't get motivated for these lesser tournaments — and yet, with his sense of self-confidence clearly wavering, he was skipping many of the biggest events on the tour!

At the U.S. Open that September, Andre narrowly missed getting thrown out of the tournament. In fact, he should have been — for spitting on the umpire's shoes. He claimed he hadn't meant to, but the re-plays showed otherwise. Luckily for Andre, he was merely fined $3,000, and was allowed to continue playing.

Andre took full advantage of the second chance he'd been given. He beat several formidable oppo-nents, including Petr Korda of Czechoslovakia, and Russia's Andrei Cherkasov. Then, in the semis, he ran into Boris Becker.

Becker had won the tournament the year before and was favored to win it again. The first set took more than an hour, with a 22-point tie-breaker, and Becker came away victorious. In the past, Andre Agassi would have folded up and gone down to easy defeat. But not this day. Andre came back to win the match, 6−7, 6−3, 6−2, 6−3, handling Becker easily. After the final point, he fell to his knees in prayer, on the exact spot where he'd spat on the official's shoes ten days before.

For the second time in four months, Andre Agassi went into a Grand Slam final, favored by the odds-makers to win. This time, he was also the favorite of the New York fans, the glamorous guy from Vegas. He went against little-known Pete Sampras.

Unlike Andre, Sampras was quiet and polite, only twenty years old, one year younger than Andre. If he won, he'd be the youngest-ever winner of the U.S. Open.

And win he did. With his smashing serves scoring aces to every box on the court, he whipped Andre, 6−4, 6−3, 6−2. Andre called the victory lucky, but as the next few years have proved, Sampras's success was no accident. He has won several Grand Slams, proving himself to be a great champion.

And Andre? He had come so close, not once, but twice. And lost. People were now beginning to question whether he had the mental and emotional strength to win the big tournaments. Even Andre himself began to have his doubts.

Still, his near victory at Flushing Meadow won him back his spot on the Davis Cup team. Andre beat Horst Skoff of Germany, before losing to rising star Thomas Muster, 6−2, 6−2, 7−6. Luckily, the American squad won anyway, and made it to that year's final tie against Australia, in St. Petersburg, Florida.

Before that final tie, Andre flew to Frankfurt, Germany, for the ATP Tournament, where he proceeded to beat both Boris Becker and Stefan Edberg. Then he returned to the United States for the Davis Cup final and beat Australia's Richard Fromberg in five sets. The low-ranked Fromberg gave him more trouble than either Becker or Edberg, but Andre told the world that his weak performance was due to a case of the flu.

After that, things went quickly downhill. The Americans had already won the Cup when Andre stepped onto the court against Darren Cahill for the final match. After each player had won a set, Andre gave up, claiming a pulled chest muscle. Was he really injured, or did he just not feel like playing, since the Cup was already won?

No one will ever know. But the angry whispers grew louder. Andre skipped the last tournament of the year — the Grand Slam Cup, for the year's best players. For that, the ITF fined him $25,000 — pocket change for Agassi, who had already won $1,741,382 that year on the circuit, not to mention the advertising deals, which continued to pour in.

In all, 1990 had been a good year for Andre: He'd reached his first two Grand Slam finals, won four individual titles, and helped the United States to the Davis Cup. He finished the year ranked 4th, up from 7th the year before. But he'd still been maddeningly inconsistent, and his fans wondered when he'd win that first coveted Grand Slam title.

It wasn't going to be at the 1991 Australian Open, that was for sure. Once again, Andre decided to skip the trip down under. When he did return to the court, he lost in successive tournaments to Brad Gilbert, Christian Saceanu (number 153 in the world), Jim Courier, and David Wheaton — all in the first round!

It was at this point that Andre broke up with Amy Moss and reunited with Wendy Stewart. The change seemed to have a good effect on him, because he went on to win the Orlando Classic that week. Then he was off to the French Open, where once again, after beating Boris Becker in the semis, he made it to the finals, and to a match against his old nemesis, Jim Courier. The match drew much attention, particularly since Nick Bollettieri sat in his courtside box with Agassi's family, glaring at Courier.

But it was Courier who won the day. The turning point came in the second set, with Andre up a set and leading 4–1. Courier's new coach, Jose Higueras, told Jim to start standing ten feet back from the base line to return Andre's serve. It wound up being brilliant advice. Courier stormed back to win the match in five sets, outlasting Andre, 3–6, 6–4, 2–6, 6–1, 6–4, to win the French Open title.

It was a crushing defeat for Andre. He had now lost not one, not two, but three straight Grand Slam finals. Those who said he didn't have it in him to win the big ones were now more sure of it than ever. Andre, they said, didn't have the mental toughness to win the critical matches. Andre was half inclined to agree with them, but he wasn't going to accept that image of himself without a fight. He announced to the world that he would be going to Wimbledon.

The world held its breath. How would Andre, with his multicolored outfits, deal with Wimbledon's "white-only" dress code? How would his foul language and bad manners go over in the palace of politeness that was the All England Club?

As it turned out, Andre surprised and pleased everyone when he appeared on Centre Court. Peeling off his track suit, he revealed a stylish, all-white outfit that featured shiny white cycling shorts under white tennis shorts. He also played well enough to beat Canada's Grant Connell, although it took him five sets. He then went on to beat Croatia's Goran Prpic to make it to the third round.

Through it all, his manners were impeccable, his charisma on display. And the crowd loved him! By the time he went down in the quarterfinals to David Wheaton, he had succeeded in winning over the British tennis public completely.

For his part, Andre felt the magic spell of Wimbledon. It had tamed his rebellious side and allowed him to get into the spirit of the place. "I can't wait for next year," he said afterward. "This is definitely my all-time favorite place in the whole world."

His inspiration carried over to the Washington Classic, which he won two weeks later. But soon after that, the inspiration ran out. As before, Andre didn't seem to be able to work himself up to play his best tennis in the lesser tournaments. He suffered successive losses, to Brad Gilbert, Petr Korda, Fabrice Santoro of France, and Goran Ivanisevic.

Then came the U.S. Open. The tennis world had its eyes on Agassi, to see how he would do one year after making the final. Was he finally ready to make his long-awaited breakthrough in a Grand Slam?

No. Playing poorly, he was bumped in the first round, in straight sets, by fellow Bollettieri grad Aaron Krickstein. Andre couldn't believe it, and neither could anyone else. It was a devastating loss.

Andre did manage to rouse himself briefly for the Davis Cup semifinals against Germany, beating Michael Stich and Eric Jelen. In the finals against France, in Lyon, Andre did his part, beating Guy Forget in four sets. But the American team was outplayed by the inspired home team, and lost the Cup 3–1.

Though 1991 ended with Andre a million dollars richer from tennis earnings alone, he was not happy. Money was not everything. He wanted a Grand Slam title, and it seemed like he would never get one.

Already, Michael Chang, Jim Courier, and Pete Sampras had won Grand Slams. Andre had been more highly touted than any of them, and yet they had all reached that goal before him.

He finished the year ranked 10th, a real comedown from the year before. He was only twenty-one — still young — but he was tired, discouraged, and lost. At home, he quarreled with his dad. He was tired of hearing Mike Agassi's endless suggestions. "Why should I listen to you?" Andre snapped. He moved out and found a house of his own nearby.

But the move didn't seem to help, any more than anything else had. The year 1992 started out poorly. After skipping the Australian Open yet again, Andre went on to lose to a string of lesser players in early rounds of smaller tournaments: Jakob Hlasek of Switzerland in Milan, Alexander Volkov of Russia in Brussels, Marc Rosset of Switzerland in Scottsdale, Jacco Eltingh of the Netherlands in Barcelona, and Franco Davin of Argentina in Tampa.

After this series of losses, the French Open loomed in front of him like a dark, threatening cloud. Andre remembered back one year. Jim Courier had beaten him in the finals. Ever since that match, his game had pretty well gone to pieces. Could he put it back together again?

From the moment he walked out onto the court at Roland Garros, the magic was back. The young people in the crowd adored him, the older fans hated him, but no one could take their eyes off him. Andre, his hair in its trademark peroxide ponytail, his outfits each more outrageous than the next, his on-court antics constant, breezed through his first five matches, losing only one set on his way to the finals.

There, he was paired against none other than Jim Courier, the reigning champion. Mike Agassi was in the stands. So was Bollettieri. Andre was about to get his revenge, they were sure of it.

From the first shot, Courier was on the offensive. Andre was thrown totally off balance. At this time, Courier was showing the form that would soon see him ranked number 1 in the world. It was no contest. Andre went down, 3–6, 2–6, 2–6. Bollettieri held his head in his hands in anguish.

That week, the headlines read "Agassi — A Born Loser?" Wimbledon was coming up. Would Andre show up? And if he did, which Agassi would it be?

Chapter Ten
June 1992

The Most Incredible Moment

Andre was in the worst slump of his career. At times it seemed like he'd grown used to losing and accepted it. Then, just when everyone was counting him out, he'd come back and win a tournament, playing his best tennis. When Andre was "on," no one returned a second serve as well as he did.

The second serve is generally the shortest shot in tennis, and it's the perfect moment to smash a winning ground stroke. That was Andre Agassi's tennis game, and nobody could do it better — sometimes.

Recently, Andre had been showing the world what he was capable of, and then "choking in the clutch," failing to play his best tennis at the most important times. Would this happen again at Wimbledon?

Wimbledon favored big players with huge

serves — people like Boris Becker, Stefan Edberg, Michael Stich, Richard Krajicek, and Pete Sampras, all of whom had won the tournament before 1992, or have won it since. They play a "serve and volley" game, running up to the net to follow up their big serves.

Andre Agassi was not that type of player. He was smallish, at five-eleven and 165 pounds. Andre's game consisted of staying back at the baseline and smashing killer returns.

To most observers, Wimbledon's grass didn't seem like the ideal surface for Agassi. But Andre didn't see it that way. To him, the magic was in this place, this tennis stadium, with all its history and the crowd so quiet and polite you'd think you were at church.

The year 1992 would mark the 106th Wimbledon Championship. After the French Open two weeks before, played on slow clay, most of the players rushed off to get some practice on grass. But Andre simply went to Las Vegas and reminded himself that he had a home.

He thought he could win. In fact, he thought he might have won the year before if his thigh muscle hadn't acted up on him in the middle of his quarterfinal match with David Wheaton. He'd been leading Wheaton at the time, two sets to one. If he hadn't run into bad luck . . .

The place brought out Andre's spiritual side, which strengthened his inner game. He came to Wimbledon mentally ready to win in the crunch. He felt he was poised to finally become a Grand Slam champion.

His opening match was against the Russian Andrei Chesnekov — a bad break right off the bat. Chesnekov was an inconsistent player who had streaks where he was almost unbeatable.

Andre had trouble with the Russian, who was definitely on his game. Rain interrupted the match, and they had to finish it the next day. In the end, Andre managed to escape with a nerve-racking 5–7, 6–1, 7–5, 7–5 win.

Andre felt lucky to have survived into the second round at Wimbledon. His fans were supporting him 100 percent — yet they were perplexed by something. Why was Andre, the "Image Is Everything" man, wearing a cap out onto the court? Why was he hiding his gorgeous hair all of a sudden?

The truth was, Andre was starting to lose his hair

a little. He insisted he had worn the hat because it was a lucky hat, though, not to hide anything. But the newspapers had a field day over Andre's disappearing hair anyway.

Andre stepped onto the court against Belgium's Eduardo Masso without the hat, just to prove the hair was still practically all there. But when he lost the first set, he immediately put the cap back on, after which he went on to win easily. So much for playing without his lucky cap!

In the third round, Andre got by Derrick Rostagno in straight sets. That led to a fourth-round match with Germany's Christian Saceanu. Saceanu had come out of nowhere, and was no easy opponent. Andre beat him, 7–6, 6–1, 7–6, in a straight set match that featured two tie-breakers. Agassi won them both. In fact, he was winning many big points in his matches. People began to take notice. Had Agassi learned to fight to the end instead of giving up?

In the quarterfinals, Boris Becker loomed. Becker called Wimbledon his "back garden." He had been champion here three times, and had reached the final in six of the last seven years. Surely he would tame the wild man from Las Vegas. Andre had gotten by some "easy" opponents, spectators said, but "Boom-Boom" Becker would be too much for Agassi.

Becker's huge serve won him the first set, 6–4. But Agassi came back, with a succession of fierce forehand and backhand baseline passing shots, to win the next two sets, 6–2, 6–2. Then darkness fell, and the rains came. The next day the match resumed. Becker played brilliantly, using his classic serve-and-volley game to take the fourth set, 6–4.

The German continued to serve wonderfully in the fifth and final set. But Andre Agassi was standing back at the baseline, returning those smashing serves with ease, sending them back across the net as unreturnable winners. The set was 5–1 Agassi before Becker could recover. He edged up to 5–3 by breaking Andre's serve.

But it was too late. On Andre's next service, he put the match away. Andre Agassi was now officially "for real." The Wimbledon favorites watched, and worried. "You cannot play better tennis than he did on grass that day," Becker said afterward, amazed that he'd been beaten at Wimbledon on a day when he'd played his best.

Andre found himself in the Wimbledon semifinals

after his great victory over Becker. His opponent was none other than John McEnroe, his Davis Cup teammate, his doubles partner, his friend.

When he'd first met Andre, McEnroe couldn't stand him. Perhaps Andre's fits of temper reminded him unpleasantly of his own. But over time, the two had grown close. They'd discovered they respected each other and had a lot in common.

McEnroe was the crowd favorite in this tournament, the old lion back for one more run at the trophy. But Andre was the one with the bite, bringing McEnroe to ground, 6–4, 6–2, 6–3. He had made the final!

Andre Agassi had been to Grand Slam finals before — twice in Paris and once at the U.S. Open — and all three times, he had lost. The night before his Wimbledon final he went outside the All England Club and sat on a hilltop, staring across London at a distant church steeple.

This was it, he thought. Tomorrow he'd either be a Grand Slam champion or a four-time loser. If he lost, Andre thought, he might just quit tennis forever. All his life, he'd worked so hard to become the best he could be. Constantly losing when he

87

was so near the top was too painful. It was now or never.

The next day, Andre faced Goran Ivanisevic of Croatia, a man who could fire 140-mile-per-hour serves all day long, sometimes with deadly accuracy. He would go on streaks where he was just unhittable. In this very tournament, he'd already destroyed Stefan Edberg, Ivan Lendl, and Pete Sampras.

The first set was a marathon, lasting forty-one minutes, with an 18-point tie-breaker finally deciding the outcome. Ivanisevic ended up winning on one of his many aces. Andre was down, 6–7. After all that effort, he had come away empty.

But the match was not over, and Andre swore to himself he would not give in until the last point was won. He stormed back to take the next two sets with astonishing returns and passing shots. But in the fourth set his concentration deserted him and Ivanisevic evened the match, 6–7, 6–4, 6–4, 1–6.

In the fifth and final set, the score went to 3–3 without either player having a clear advantage. Then Andre went behind, 30–40, on his own serve. If he lost the next point, it could mean losing the match. His fans held their breath.

His first serve went wide. But his second was gorgeous, and he followed Ivanisevic's return with a fantastic volley that won the point.

Andre soon led 5–4. It was Ivanisevic's turn to serve. Andre had not broken the Croatian's serve for two whole sets. Would the fifth and final match go to another tie-breaker?

But suddenly, at the critical moment, it was Ivanisevic, not Andre, who faltered. He double-faulted twice, and then yet again on match point!

It was over. Andre had won! He sank to his hands and knees, overcome by emotion. "Stay down!" Bollettieri yelled, always mindful of the news photographers. But Andre didn't need to be told. He couldn't have stood up just then if his life had depended on it.

Finally, image *wasn't* everything. The tennis player had come to the fore and shown what was really inside him. The heart of a champion.

Chapter Eleven
July 1992–1993

From the Highs to the Lows

When Andre drove away from the All England Tennis Club a champion, he was on top of the world. Unfortunately, there is only one way to go when you're on top — down. So the hard part is to stay right where you are, even with everybody aiming at you.

Nick Bollettieri felt vindicated, proved right for his long-suffering faith in Andre. Wendy Stewart felt the same way. As for Mike Agassi, he proceeded to tell his son just how and why he had lost the fourth set to Ivanisevic.

Now that Andre had reached the top of the tennis world, he decided it was time to get the rest of his life in order. He entertained dozens of new commercial offers. He was mobbed by crowds everywhere he went. And he proceeded to lose his very next match, just a week after winning Wimbledon.

That defeat woke Andre up, at least briefly. The next week, he won the Canadian Open by beating Ivan Lendl. But following that victory, he went into a tailspin. He lost matches to Jaime Yzaga, Nicklas Kulti, Patrick Kuhnen, Brad Gilbert, Marc Rosset, Richard Krajicek, Sergi Bruguera, Carl-Uwe Steeb, Aaron Krickstein, Todd Martin, Michael Chang, Andrei Medvedev, and Thomas Enqvist. In that year's U.S. Open, he was bounced in the quarter finals.

Andre managed to win only two more minor tournaments the rest of that year, in San Francisco and Scottsdale, Arizona. He did play well, as always, on the Davis Cup team, helping the United States win 1992's Cup. But even then, he caused a big upset by threatening to quit the team if McEnroe wasn't appointed the next year's coach. (He wasn't. Andre played anyway.)

Andre finished the year ranked number 9, only one higher than the year before, in spite of his Wimbledon triumph. He was in a slump he just couldn't seem to get out of, and his life off the court was proving to be just as pressure-filled. Social and business obligations were overwhelming him, making it difficult for him to focus on identifying why his game was going downhill.

When he again refused to play in the Australian Open — for the sixth straight time — people could only shake their heads. Was Andre Agassi simply a one-hit wonder? Then Andre came back to win events in San Francisco and Scottsdale in February, the eighteenth and nineteenth titles of his career. That silenced his critics for a while.

But then something happened that sent Andre into another tailspin. Wendy Stewart, his longtime love, broke up with him once and for all. She wanted to remain friends, but she said his constant traveling, his mood swings, having to watch him always surrounded by beautiful girls, had finally grown too much for her to bear.

Andre was hard hit by Wendy's announcement, and drowned his sorrow by eating junk food. By early 1993 he had gained quite a bit of weight and was definitely out of shape.

There were even more troubles ahead for Andre. During a quarterfinal loss in the Barcelona Open in April, Andre felt pain in his right wrist. People thought he was just making excuses again. They said

Andre was hiding out because he'd been losing ever since Wimbledon. When Andre skipped the French Open, a tournament he'd always done well in, they should have realized he wasn't faking it.

But the whispers grew ever louder, and many people wondered if Andre would show up at Wimbledon to defend his title. When he lost the week before in a grass-court warmup, looking bad going down in defeat to Carl-Uwe Steeb, most people were betting Andre would stay away.

He showed up after all, with his wrist heavily taped. His body hair had been shaved to make him "more aerodynamic," but he was sporting about twenty extra pounds. He had a famous new girlfriend — none other than singer Barbra Streisand, who called her new beau a "Zen master," for his incredible abilities on the court. But whatever Barbra's opinion, the experts figured Agassi would go down in the first round without even putting up a fight. He might be the defending champion, but he certainly hadn't played — or behaved — like a champion in the year since he'd won.

Andre stepped out onto Centre Court, and was greeted by a roaring standing ovation. Whatever the experts were saying, the Wimbledon crowd hadn't forgotten the Agassi who had won their hearts with his brilliant play the year before.

Andre was touched by the magic of their approval. He stormed through his first-round match, beating Bernd Karbacher of Germany, 7–5, 6–4, 6–0. He continued to dazzle the crowd and the experts with his play and made it to the quarterfinals. But in the end, he just couldn't maintain the energy that had led him to the championship the year before. He finally bowed out in five amazing sets to Pete Sampras, who went on to win the championship.

Andre had played well, on sheer heart and nerve, his wrist painful, his stamina weak. The extra weight, and the wrist tendinitis, continued to take their toll on his tennis for the remainder of 1993. He played in only thirteen events that year, winning just the two early singles titles and one doubles title (with Petr Korda in Cincinnati). In the U.S. Open, he was beaten in the first round by Thomas Enqvist.

But the worst blow to Andre's 1993 season was both personal and professional. After Wimbledon, he had heard rumors that Nick Bollettieri had decided to leave him. Andre couldn't believe it! After all the time they'd spent together, after Andre had won at Wimbledon the year before? Finally, in a long letter, Bollettieri admitted that, yes, he was severing the relationship. He said he needed to spend more time with his family. But Andre soon found out the truth, along with everybody else. Believing that Agassi was through, burned-out, finished, Bollettieri had deserted him to become Boris Becker's coach.

"He's a selfish person," Andre remarked bitterly to the press. "He thought that I wasn't going to do well anymore. But he didn't have the guts to tell it like it was."

Bollettieri's departure could have been the final nail in the coffin for Andre's tennis career. Certainly, 1993 had been a nightmare year for Agassi. But he wasn't willing to give up. Not yet.

Chapter Twelve
1993–1994

Eyes on the Prize

When Andre got back to Las Vegas in 1993, many of his friends, even his brother, Phil, wondered if he would ever get back to the form that had made him such a feared tennis player. So much had gone wrong for Andre since his Wimbledon win. He was fifteen pounds overweight; he was depressed, unmotivated, and in emotional and physical pain. He needed surgery on his wrist.

No one would have blamed him if he had hung up his racket and tennis shoes forever. At twenty-three, he had enough money to keep him more than comfortable for the rest of his life. Beautiful women surrounded him wherever he went, fans adored him, companies threw money at him to endorse their products. It didn't seem to matter much whether he won or lost.

Andre wrestled with himself, trying to discover whether, deep inside, he still had the desire to play. He spent time alone, trying to answer that most important of questions for himself. He entered psychotherapy, and spent eight months looking over his life, his childhood, and his relationships with his father and Bollettieri.

He began to realize that both men had made their love for him dependent on whether he won at tennis. If he lost, he got the cold shoulder. If he won, he got a hug. Andre had been playing tennis to please everyone but the person who mattered most — himself.

He thought back to his earliest childhood days, when his dad had put those first rackets in his hands. Andre had really loved the game, and not just because his dad pushed it on him. Now, he began to reach back and connect with that love.

He let himself feel the pain of being rejected by his "step-dad," Bollettieri. He began to look around and see who in his life he could depend on the most. The answer was clear: Phil, Perry Rogers, his trainer Gil Reyes, his old friends, his family — even his dad.

He saw the movie *Shadowlands*, about the life of the writer C. S. Lewis, and was struck by Lewis's emotional awakening. "The pain then is part of the happiness now," Lewis had said. Andre began to believe that he, too, could come to feel that way.

He began reading Lewis's books, and loved them. He read Marianne Williamson's and Tony Robbins's self-improvement books, and even had private sessions with Williamson and Robbins. Andre was determined to do anything to turn his life around.

Gil Reyes put him on a regimen of diet and exercise. No more goofing off. Andre had to do sit-ups, weight lifting, stair stepping — all kinds of exercise except those involving his wrist — for two and a half hours a day, six days a week, week after week.

There was no more junk food, either. In what must have felt like the biggest sacrifice of his life, Andre Agassi gave up doughnuts, tacos, fries, burgers, chicken wings, and thick shakes. He began to treat his body with respect . . . and his body began to respond. He went from 180 pounds to a sleek, muscular 165.

Even though Andre had temporarily left the tennis scene, he was still as wildly popular as ever. Wherever he went, fans pursued him. Companies still paid him millions to help sell their products — his business interests were now looked after by Agassi Enterprises, headed by Perry Rogers.

In fact, Andre no longer really needed to play tennis for the money. But just at the crucial moment, he had found another reason to play — the overwhelming desire to be the best in the world at the game he loved so much.

Andre was about to find love in another area as well. One day, an unexpected fax came in on the machine in Andre's office. It was a letter from Africa, from actress Brooke Shields, one of the most famous, most beautiful women in the world.

The letter was light and funny, joking around about how she was bored to tears on the set of the movie she was filming in the jungle. Brooke had been persuaded to write to Andre, just for something to do, by the wife of rocker Kenny G, who was a mutual friend of Shields and Agassi. What Brooke didn't expect was the reply she got from Andre. It was a passionate outpouring of all his deepest feelings. His letter talked about how important it was to be vulnerable, to stay open, not to close up when you were in pain — all the lessons he had learned in the past couple of months.

Brooke was stunned. She saw that Andre was a lot like her. He was the child of a fanatical parent (Brooke's mother had driven her to be a model and actress), wildly famous and mobbed by fans wherever he went, and, like her, was desperately seeking privacy and understanding. Before she knew what was happening, Brooke Shields found herself falling for Andre — a guy she'd never even met face to face!

They finally did meet, in December of 1993, when Brooke's movie was finished and she returned to the States. Before his surgery, the two went out to a restaurant on their first date. Seeing the long-haired Andre only from behind, a waitress said, "Are you two ladies enjoying your dinner?" What a surprise that waitress got when Andre turned around!

On that first date, Andre didn't even kiss Brooke. She was surprised at how gentle and polite he was, how understanding and down-to-earth.

Soon after that, Andre took five months off from the tennis tour to have surgery on his wrist. Then it was Brooke's turn. She needed an operation on her foot to repair damage from dancing. While she lay in her hospital bed recovering, Andre was at her side constantly. Brooke wasn't looking or feeling her best, but his attraction to her, she saw, wasn't because she was beautiful on the outside. It made her love him even more.

She saw how generous he was. Andre had bought houses and cars for the people he loved, lavishing gifts on them whenever the mood struck him. He was loyal, too. His friends were his friends for life.

As for Andre, he felt that Brooke was perfect for him. Rather than being someone who was jealous of his great fame, Brooke had great fame herself. She had a career of her own that kept her traveling around the world, just as he did. She was intelligent, vulnerable, and open. And Brooke and Andre were at a similar point in their lives. They wanted more than anything else to live up to their great gifts, to be more than just image.

At the end of 1993, Andre Agassi's ranking in the tennis computer was a lowly 24. By February, after skipping the Australian Open yet again, he had slipped all the way to number 32. But Andre didn't let that bother him. With his wrist on the mend and

Brooke in his life, he felt sure he was ready for another comeback, greater than any before. He promised himself he would never let up until he was number 1 in the world.

Andre had found a new direction. He had taken a good look at himself, then made himself better. He had love in his life, and had found his missing love for tennis. There was only one thing more he needed to reach the top — a new coach. Since Bollettieri had dumped him, Andre had tried working with Pancho Segura, but the relationship did not work out.

At the start of 1994, Andre once again found himself looking for a new coach. Surprisingly, the person he wound up finding was Brad Gilbert. Brad was only nine years older than Andre, and he was still a player on the tour himself. He had once been ranked in the top 10, but only for a short while. Most of the time, he'd been less than world-class.

But Brad Gilbert had something that neither of Andre's other coaches had: experience on the court against the very same players Andre faced. Gilbert was a smart player who had won many matches he shouldn't have won, against more talented players, including Andre Agassi.

Andre took Gilbert out to dinner and asked him for his honest opinion of his tennis game. What were the weaknesses? Where did he need to improve? Gilbert didn't hold back. He thought Andre wasn't using his head to win tennis matches. Agassi needed to think through the whole game. He needed to play stronger second sets, not give them up easily to save his energy for a desperate comeback later. He needed to become more consistent, more feared on the court, to serve bigger and come forward more, so he could dictate play.

Andre was impressed with what — and how much — Gilbert had to say. The two men agreed to a trial partnership. If it worked out, Gilbert would become Andre's permanent coach.

Andre had already shown some signs of a turnaround when he met with Gilbert. In February, he had won a tournament in Scottsdale without losing a single set. Now, with Gilbert at his side, he went into the Lipton Championships in Key Biscayne, Florida. It was a tournament where all the big names came to play.

The new Andre Agassi electrified the crowd. He was still the same flamboyant showman, with his blond ponytail, earrings, and outrageous out-fits — but his tennis was amazing. He was playing better than he had in years, maybe better than he ever had!

In the third round, he came up against Boris Becker, Nick Bollettieri's new prize pupil. It was time for sweet revenge. To the wild cheers of the crowd, Andre took Becker apart, using all the pointers Brad Gilbert had given him. At one point, the German star got so upset with himself for not knowing how to handle the new, improved Agassi that he gave his racket to one of the ball girls, Stephanie Flaherty.

Agassi called out, "Stephanie! Come on!" inviting her onto the court and playing a point with her! The crowd went berserk. Their Andre was back, and he was giving them a great performance.

After beating Becker, 6–2, 7–5, Andre dispensed with Cedric Pioline of France, 6–4, 6–2. Then he beat Stefan Edberg, ranked number 3 in the world, 7–6, 6–2. By this time, everyone knew that Andre Agassi had been reborn.

Andre went into the final against Pete Sampras on a roll. And luck seemed to be smiling on him, too. Sampras awoke that morning with an upset stomach.

He let the judges know that he could not make it to the final by 1 P.M., the scheduled time for the match.

All Andre had to do was show up and win by forfeit. But this was a new Andre Agassi. He wanted to win — more than ever — but not like that. Showing tremendous class and generosity, he asked the match officials to push the match back an hour so Sampras could see a doctor and be treated. "Pete can take as much time as he needs," Andre said. "I don't want to win this way."

Sampras was so impressed by Andre's gesture that he has never forgotten it. To this day, he has a great respect and admiration for Agassi.

But he didn't let such feelings get in the way once the match began. Sampras, then rated number 1 in the world, proceeded to end Andre's winning streak, 5–7, 6–3, 6–3.

Andre did not regret what he had done. Even though he didn't win the tournament, he knew he had done the right thing. He had played well enough to raise his ranking from number 32 to number 20. He had shown his opponents that he wasn't washed up — in fact, he was better than ever. It was only a hint of much greater things to come.

Chapter Thirteen
June–September 1994

Image Is *Not* Everything

The first major tournament in May 1994 was the French Open. Even though Andre lost in the second round to Thomas Muster of Germany, he was clearly playing a stronger, more consistent game of tennis. Brad Gilbert watched from the stands, taking notes to refine Andre's game even further. Wimbledon was next.

Andre showed up with newly shaved legs, but without Brooke Shields, who had also missed the French Open. Were the two still a couple? More than ever, Andre told the press. Brooke just didn't want to be a distraction for Andre. She wanted him to be able to concentrate on his tennis during the Grand Slam tournaments.

In the second round, he endured a brief scare from Nicolas Pereira of Venezuela, finally beating him in five sets with a great last-minute comeback, 6–7, 6–3, 6–4, 6–7, 6–4. Aaron Krickstein, fellow Bollettieri graduate, was Andre's next victim. That got him into a fourth-round match with Todd Martin, the "Most Improved Player" on the circuit that year.

Martin was six feet six and a wickedly powerful server, which is an advantage at Wimbledon, with its fast grass. A big server on his game can wipe out anybody in the world there. Against Agassi, Martin was unbeatable, hitting so many aces and service winners in the fifth and final set that Andre couldn't keep up.

It wasn't a bad showing at Wimbledon, but it wasn't a title either. Still, Andre didn't let himself get discouraged. His new path, he was sure, would lead him to the top of the tennis world.

He went to the Canadian Open the following week and won the tournament, beating up-and-coming Australian Jason Stoltenberg in the final. That victory was the beginning of a dazzling run of tennis for Andre.

September came, and with it the U.S. Open. Andre had risen to number 20 in the rankings, but still entered the Open as an unseeded player. First seed belonged to Pete Sampras, still number 1 in the world after his second straight Wimbledon title.

Andre arrived on-court for his first-round match, with Sweden's Robert Eriksson, wearing new Nike tennis shoes with bulbous blue fronts that looked like they had been made for Minnie Mouse. Andre stared across the court at his opponent, ready to make a statement to the world. He felt in his heart that up to now, he had wasted much of his talent because he hadn't had enough self-discipline. That was over now. He was ready.

Eriksson went down without much of a fight, 6–3, 6–2, 6–0. More important, Boris Becker and Goran Ivanisevic also lost their first-round matches. Without these opponents to face, Andre's chances were a little better.

Guy Forget of France was Andre's next victim, followed by Wayne Ferreira of South Africa. Then, in round four, he came face to face with Michael Chang.

The match went on for five long, grueling sets. In the old days, by the end of the three-hour match Andre would have run out of energy and lost. But this time, it was Chang who tired first, as the new, more fit Agassi overwhelmed him in the final set, 6–1, 6–7, 6–3, 3–6, 6–1.

The victory over Chang convinced Andre that he could go all the way and win the tournament he'd wanted to win for so long. The crowd now seemed to be convinced, too. Their hero, Sampras, had gone down in the fourth round to the much smaller, lower-rated Jaime Yzaga of Peru, 3–6, 6–3, 4–6, 7–6, 7–5. Unknown to the fans, Sampras had been playing on a bad ankle for some time. Added to that, he was exhausted, and was nursing blisters on his feet. He limped badly through the last set, using his racket as a cane. He showed great heart and courage, but in the end, he could not go on.

The fans now turned their attention — and affection — to Agassi. He made them happy by winning his quarterfinal match with Thomas Muster, the man who'd knocked him out of the French Open.

He followed that victory with an even sweeter bit of payback, a win in the semifinals over Todd Martin, his Wimbledon conqueror, 6–3, 4–6, 6–2, 6–3. During this match, Andre's serve amazed both the spectators and his opponent. Andre showed a degree of power and accuracy none of them had ever seen in his service game before.

Michael Stich of Germany, six feet four inches tall,

was the only one who stood between Andre Agassi and glory on that perfect Sunday afternoon. Stich was also having an incredible run — but only one player would win the trophy that day.

Before the match, Andre had told Brad Gilbert, "There's no way Stich is leaving here with my title." On the court, he unleashed screaming winner after screaming winner. He lost only 17 points on his own serve. And he had Stich reeling from the first, winning the first set 6–1 before the German knew what hit him.

With his legion of fans — this time including Brooke Shields — shouting, "Pump it up, Andre!" from the stands, Agassi held on to win in straight sets, 6–1, 7–6, 7–5. When Stich's last return clipped the top of the net but failed to go over, Andre sank to his knees, at last the winner of the coveted U.S. Open. He was the first unseeded player to win the tournament in almost thirty years. "I can't believe it!" he cried. But it was true.

He ran to the stands to kiss Brooke, then took his trophy, kissed it, too, and held it high over his head. No one could doubt him — or stop him — now.

Chapter Fourteen
October 1994–1995

On Top of the World

Andre's phenomenal run continued after the U.S. Open; he went on to win tour events in Toronto and Paris. By the end of 1994, he had beaten every player in the top 10, and had risen from number 32 to number 2 in one unbelievable year.

For Christmas, he and Brooke celebrated in a rather unusual way. They had a hairdresser come up to her apartment in New York City and cut off Andre's ponytail! Andre had been losing a lot of hair, and both agreed he would look better with his hair cut very short. As for the ponytail, it went straight to a bank vault, where it was held for safekeeping. Soon it would be hung on the wall at the All-Star Cafe, a new restaurant chain of which Andre was now part-owner.

He also became a much wealthier man, when

Perry Rogers negotiated a new ten-year deal for him with Nike — for $100 million dollars!

In January 1995, for the very first time, Andre entered the Australian Open. Eighteen of the top twenty players in the world were there. But after the U.S. Open, Brad Gilbert had assured Andre he could win in Australia. Andre was confident he could pull it off, too.

The fans couldn't believe it when the new Andre Agassi stepped out onto Centre Court. He had his hair cut short, no ponytail, with a pirate's earring and bandanna. The crowd dubbed him "The Black Prince," and Andre soon showed them that his tennis was as fierce as his look.

He drubbed Grant Stafford of South Africa, Jerome Golmard of France, and Greg Rusedski of Canada to make it into the fourth round. Here, he faced popular local hero Patrick Rafter, who made the girls swoon even more than Andre did. But Rafter was no match for Agassi on the court, losing 6–3, 6–4, 6–0.

Yevgeny Kafelnikov of Russia was next, waiting for Andre in the quarterfinals. He was worried, and rightly so. Andre took him apart in eighty-three minutes to advance into the semifinals, where he met Aaron Krickstein.

All this time, Andre had been pretty much alone. He had arrived in Melbourne with only Brad Gilbert and his trainer, Gil Reyes. Brooke was back in New York, starring as Rizzo in the Broadway musical *Grease*. The three men rented a private bungalow just outside of town, where they spent the evenings between matches — not partying, just sitting at home watching action movies.

The videos put Andre in a pumped-up, primed-for-action mood. Krickstein was dispatched in straight sets, 6–4, 6–4, 3–0. In the middle of the third set, Krickstein strained his groin and had to give up. Andre was into the final — without losing a single set the whole tournament!

His opponent would be Pete Sampras. It was to be a classic matchup between number 1 in the world versus Andre's number 2. Sampras, in spite of his stomach ailment, had beaten Andre the last time they'd met. Had Andre improved to the point where he could now beat the number 1 player in the world?

Sampras had been through a lot since the two had last met. He had lost in the U.S. Open because of a foot injury. That was healed now, but Sampras was still not back to his old stamina level. On top of that, his coach and closest friend, Tim Gullickson, had collapsed earlier in the Australian tournament and been taken back to the United States. (The illness, unfortunately, turned out to be a fatal brain tumor. Gullickson died in 1996.)

During his semifinal match with Jim Courier, Sampras started thinking of his missing coach, and broke down sobbing right there on Centre Court. The fans were aghast. "You all right, Pete?" Courier called out. "We can come back and do this tomorrow." His words seemed to snap Sampras out of it. He went back to the baseline and served. Soon he had won the match, in five sets, 6–7, 6–7, 6–3, 6–3, 6–4. It was a tremendous display of courage.

Now he and Andre stood face to face. The fans were on the edge of their seats. Sampras won the first set, 6–4. But Agassi sensed that his opponent was faltering. Andre came back to whip Sampras, 6–1, in the second set.

It was one set apiece. But Andre was not to be stopped. He fired twenty-eight aces, while Sampras, tired and disheartened, committed fifty unforced errors. Andre won the next two sets, 7–6, and 6–4.

After skipping the Australian Open for seven straight years, Andre Agassi had come, he had seen, and he had conquered. Andre held up his second straight Grand Slam trophy and smiled at the crowd.

On April 10, 1995, Andre Agassi achieved his life-long dream: he captured the number 1 ranking for the first time. He was the best men's tennis player in the world!

Chapter Fifteen
1995–1996

Number 1 and Beyond

The Agassi-Sampras rivalry would go on throughout 1995. The two met four more times that year. At Indian Wells, Sampras won. Andre took their matches in Key Biscayne and Montreal, Canada. Sampras won the last match, the final of the U.S. Open.

Perhaps the greatest year of Andre's career was 1995 — certainly it was his best since 1988. He was the most consistent player on the men's tour, with a match record of 73 and 9. He was ranked number 1 every week from April 10 to November 5, when Sampras took it back.

Andre won seven titles out of eleven finals that year. He reached the finals in all ten hard-court tournaments he entered. In many of those matches, he faced the best players in the game. He won in Washington, beating Edberg; in Cincinnati, defeating Chang; in Montreal, winning over Sampras; and in New Haven, getting by Krajicek.

In all of 1995, Andre didn't lose once in an opening-round match, a feat accomplished by no other player on the tour that year. He also had the longest winning streak of his entire career, going twenty-six matches without a defeat, before Sampras finally beat him at the U.S. Open. Andre won thirteen Davis Cup matches in a row, leading the U.S. to the final. For the year, he earned a career-high $2,975,738 playing tennis.

Andre had changed a bit. He was still generous with his friends and family, lavishing gifts on them, building them houses next to his in a giant family compound in Las Vegas. But Andre now limited himself to just $150,000 a year spending money. He was no longer the extravagant spender, at least not on himself.

Much of his money went to charity. Since the beginning, Andre Agassi had given his time, energy, and money to various good causes. For instance, in 1994 he donated $1 million dollars to renovate a local Boys and Girls Club in his hometown of Las Vegas.

During the off-season, Andre proposed to Brooke Shields. She accepted, and he gave her an engagement ring. The two haven't set a definite date yet, but they agree it will be sooner rather than later.

The year 1996 started out badly for Andre — he was bounced out of the French Open in the second round by Chris Woodruff, and out of Wimbledon in the first round, by Doug Flach. By the time the Olympics rolled around he had not played very much, but he was rounding back into shape again.

Deep in his heart, Andre had always dreamed of winning Olympic gold. His father had competed in two Olympics; this was Andre's first try. He had been saying for months that the Olympics were his top priority for the year. The Games were being held on home turf, in Atlanta, Georgia. With the home crowd behind him, Andre hoped his game would come together and allow him to win a gold medal for the United States.

At the Olympics he sailed through the early rounds, and after beating Wayne Ferreira in the quarterfinals, made it into the medal round. There, he wound up in the final, against Sergi Bruguera of Spain.

In the stands sat Brooke Shields, Mike Agassi, and thousands of cheering fans chanting "U.S.A.! U.S.A.!" "Agassi Rules!" and "Viva Las Vegas!" Andre took charge of the match from the outset, hitting the ball deep and hard, always one step ahead of the Spaniard.

Bruguera began to panic, hitting unforced error after unforced error — sixty for the match in all. Andre overwhelmed him in straight sets, 6–2, 6–3, 6–1. It took him three match points to finally nail down the victory. When he did, he raised his arms jubilantly, took off his cap, bowed, and blew kisses to the fans.

Then he went over to his dad and embraced him. Andre hadn't expected Mike to be there. His dad rarely came to his matches anymore, since Andre had told him it made him nervous. But that day, Mike Agassi had flown in unannounced from Las Vegas to be with his son.

As the national anthem played and Andre stood on the medal platform, the gold around his neck, tears rolled down his cheeks.

Later he told reporters that he ranked the gold medal ahead of his three Grand Slam titles. "To win a Grand Slam in the sport of tennis is the greatest accomplishment inside the sport," he said. "To win an Olympic gold medal is the greatest thing you can accomplish in any sport."

Andre played astounding tennis during the Games. "When he's on," Bruguera said, "he's the best player in the world." In the weeks after the Olympics, Andre showed the world that that was true. Ranked number 7 in the world, he beat number 4 Yevgeny Kafelnikov, number 2 Thomas Muster, and number 3 Michael Chang, one after the other, to win the ATP Tournament in Cincinnati.

But was the former bad boy of tennis gone forever? Would Andre let his emotions get the better of him, scream at an umpire, and be thrown out of a tournament ever again?

Whether he does or not, one thing is for sure: Andre Agassi will be around, at or near the top of the tennis heap, for many years to come. And wherever he goes, whatever he does, millions of fans will watch him. He is a genuine star of the sports world. He was once number 1, and he very well may be again. And he will always be exciting to watch — on the court and off.